STREET STARS

Ray O'Brien

"Street Stars" is published by:

Trinity Mirror NW²

Trinity Mirror North West & North Wales
PO Box 48
Old Hall Street
Liverpool L69 3EB

Business Development Director:
Mark Dickinson

Business Development Executive Editor:
Ken Rogers

Written by:
Ray O'Brien

Book Editor:
Peter Grant

Design/production:
Zoë Egan, Emma Smart

ISBN 9781905266739

Thank You

Thanks are due to a number of people who have helped me with this production not least, Jim Irlam for the loan of one of the Kelly's Directories. Others who have assisted in different ways include Kevin and Pat Halpen, Kevin Roach, Liverpool City Library Record Office, Jenny Done from Wallasey Central Library, Doug Darroch, Fort Perch Rock, New Brighton, Neil Sturrock and Billy Halliday.

Thanks to Paul Melba (Francis Staunton) impressionist who appeared on the TV series The Comedians and now lives and works in Spain.

Ta to Ken Rogers for supporting the idea. Colin Hunt, Les Rawlinson and Brian Johnston and all at Trinity Mirror Sport media – Zoë Egan, Emma Smart, Lisa Critchley and Peter Grant. Stephen Shakeshaft and Eddie Barford – for their contributions too.

Also a big 'thank you' to Spencer Leigh for writing the introduction.

Foreword

By Spencer Leigh

Broadcaster and Author

So often we hear in the media that so-and-so came from Liverpool, but, of course, Liverpool is a big place and we would like to know more.

We all know where a few of our celebrities came from, but not that many, till now. Ken Dodd from Knotty Ash, Cilla Black from Scottie Road, Billy Fury from the Dingle, and John Lennon, of course, in Menlove Avenue in Woolton. Street Stars settles, once and for all, which part of Merseyside the key Liverpool celebrities were raised.

Before I read what Ray had written, I realise that there are many local stars Rita Tushingham, Arthur Askey and Kenneth Cope among them – where I have no idea where they lived.

This information comes from past Liverpool editions of Kelly's Directory as they list the householder for every property on Merseyside, which is also a most important research tool if you are researching your own family history.

But this publication is not a dry list of addresses as the celebrities are shown in photographs from the Liverpool Post and Echo's unique and wonderful archives and described in very entertaining text from Ray O'Brien.

Ray O'Brien is known for his research into Beatle sites on Merseyside and he combines historical research with a good sense of humour.

His book editior Peter Grant is a very astute writer, who has the rare ability of being able to make serious points with good jokes.

I do, however, know for certain that Roger McGough comes from Seaforth as I met him on the top of a Ribble bus when he was Number 1 with Lily The Pink.

That told me something about the way celebrity is viewed in Liverpool: one, Roger thought that there was nothing unusual in being on a bus even though he was the best-selling artist in the country, and two, other passengers also thought there was nothing unusual about Roger being on a bus and said a friendly goodbye as they got off.

Street Stars is a valuable addition to the many publications about Liverpool and Merseyside, and long may this interest in our heritage continue.

Excuse me now while I start reading. I think Kenny Everett came from Seaforth, but am I right?

Didn't Frankie Vaughan support a boys club in Great Homer Street?

Introduction

By Ray O'Brien

Local Historian and Writer

Street Stars is not intended as a definitive guide to the listed stars professional careers. Many books have already covered this aspect of their lives but it is rather an insight into their early lives before fame and fortune beckoned. Quite honestly what more can be written about the Beatles career that has not already been written ! However did you know that George Harrison once worked in a city centre store or that Arthur Askey used the same desk at the Liverpool Institute High School as Paul McCartney !

The majority of my research has been gleaned from the Kelly's (Gores) Directories which originated in Liverpool in 1766 and listed private residents and in many cases their occupations, commercial premises and educational establishments as well as many other interesting listings. With the exception of Daniel Craig and the Robbins family who are not listed all streets listed are from Kelly's. In their cases I have had to use the electoral roll.

I hope the reader will be surprised to learn that they perhaps lived in the same street as a future star or attended the same school, or worked at the same firm. My old school for instance the Liverpool Institute produced an amazing number of world famous entertainers not least Paul McCartney and George Harrison as well as the aforementioned Arthur Askey. The Menlove Avenue area bred John Lennon, Simon Rattle and Ian Broudie whilst Huyton has turned out several playwrights. It must be something in the water!

My early years were spent in Callander Road, Fairfield. I attended Boaler Street County Primary School which to the best of my knowledge did not produce any stars of the future although I do vaguely recall a classmate's father being the Liverpool comic Jimmy Coulton which we thought was quite cool at a young impressionable age! I then attended the Liverpool Institute where I would rub shoulders but not literally with future Beatles and the newscaster Peter Sissons.

I worked as a Probation Officer from 1971 to 1994 when I took early retirement leaving me time to indulge in my outside interests culminating in my writing three books about the Beatles early venues on Merseyside, several DVDS, Radio work including currently acting as an advisor on Merseybeat to a Spanish Radio station.

Merseyside is rich in talent. We are much more than football and the Beatles although their contribution is enormous, and I have attempted to include a cross section of our rich and diverse talent. The biggest difficulty was who to leave out. Enjoy !

Contents

Tom Baker	8-9	Alison Steadman	60-61
Ken Dodd	10-11	Jean Alexander	62-63
Lita Rosa	12-13	Eddie Braben	64-65
Dixie Dean	14-15	John Gorman	66-67
Ian Broudie	16-17	Robb Wilton	68-69
Ringo Starr	18-21	Brookside Close	70-71
Jimmy McGovern	22-23	Adrian Henri	72-73
Faith Brown	24-25	John Gregson	74-75
Roger McGough	26-27	Clive Hornby	76-77
Hope Street	28-29	The McGanns	78-79
Gerry Marsden	30-31	The Codmans	80-81
The Real Thing	32-33	Charlie Landsborough	82-83
John Peel	34-35	Jean Boht	84-85
Pete McGovern	36-37	Richard Stilgoe	86-87
Ian Tracey	38-39	Paul McCartney	88-91
Keith Chegwin	40-41	Holly Johnson	92-93
Alexei Sayle	42-43	Billy Butler	94-95
Billy Liddell	44-45	Rodney Street	96-99
Penny Lane	46-49	Kenneth Cope	100-101
Adrian Boult	50-51	Simon Rattle	102-103
Tom O'Connor	52-53	Bill Kenwright	104-105
John Lennon	54-57	Freddie Starr	106-107
Arthur Askey	58-59	Pauline Collins	108-109

George Harrison	110-113	Patricia Routledge	162-163
Jimmy Tarbuck	114-115	Nicholas Monsaratt	164-165
Alan Bleasdale	116-117	Tony Booth	166-167
Bold Street	118-121	Geoffrey Hughes	168-169
Alberto Remedios	122-123	Michael Holliday	170-171
Rex Harrison	124-125	Leonard Rossiter	172-173
Beryl Bainbridge	126-127	Scotland Road	174-175
Kenny Everett	128-129	Church Street	176-179
Peter Price	130-131	Alan Durband	180-181
Malandra Burrows	132-133	Billy Fury	182-183
Lime Street	134-137	Brian Jacques	184-185
Rita Tushingham	138-139	Glenda Jackson	186-187
Frankie Vaughan	140-141	Billy J.Kramer	188-189
Paul O'Grady	142-143	Anne Robinson	190-191
Stan Boardman	144-145	Les Dennis	192-193
The Robbins Family	146-147	George Melly	194-195
Lynda La Plante	148-149	Derek Nimmo	196-197
Rita Hunter	150-151	Daniel Craig	198-199
David Yip	152-153	Ricky Tomlinson	200-201
Elvis Costello	154-155	Cilla Black	202-203
Carla Lane	156-157	Brian Epstein	204-205
Mathew Street	158-161	Liverpool	206

TOM BAKER

One of the most famous faces on TV – a Scouse Doctor Who with a coloured scarf, he played the Time Lord for seven years. Actor Tom was also the voice of Little Britain.

Born on 20 January 1934 in Stanley Road, Kirkdale the eldest of three children . His father John was a Jewish sailor who spent a lot of time away and consequently it fell to his mother Mary nee Fleming a devout Catholic to bring up Thomas and his younger siblings John and Lulu. She worked as a cleaner to supplement the family income. The family moved to 4 Abbotsford Road in Norris Green and Tom was a pupil at St Mathew's Primary School and then St Swithin's in Croxteth Hall Lane.A deeply religious child it came as no surprise that

ABBOTSFORD ROAD

Cooper
Caretaker
Warehsman
Louis, motor driver
Mrs. Isabella Maud
Jinson Thos. painter
Webt Wm. warehsmn
Keeffe Wm. casual labourer
Cross Wm. Jsph. vanman
Monti Jsph
5 Doyle Jn. foreman
77 Graham Mrs. Frances
79 Burgess Chas. painter
81 Edwards Alfd. Wm. sugar refiner
83 Goad Ernest Edwd. railway porter
Sedgemoor rd

RIGHT SIDE.
2 Park Mrs. Maud Annie
4 **Baker Jn. stevedore**
6 Hart Ernest Jas. travllr
8 Mulholland Wm. Jas. telephonist
10 Sayers Mrs. Caroline
12 Mattinson Gilbt. labourer
14 Percy Edwd. shipwright

ABB
1 Wa
3 Sh
5 Ru
7 Yo
9 Ca
11 No
15 Hi
17 Ma

16 Kin
14 Ma
12 Ev
10 Kin
8 Lee
6 Mc
4 Glo
2 Da

8

on leaving school he would train to be a monk. He spent six years with the brothers of Ploemmel who were based on the Island of Jersey. He would later comment that he only became a monk because he failed the eleven plus. He has nver forgiven the Liverpool Education system and has been a life long champion of the Comprehensive system. A crisis with his faith saw him leave the brotherhood and he did his National Service with the Royal Army Medical Corps where he developed an interest in acting firstly just as a hobby.

He then spent seven months with the Merchant Navy serving on the Queen Mary. Other employment was as a clerk, hod carrier and plumbers' mate. He trained for the theatre at a speech and drama college in Kent and got his first big break with the role as Rasputin in the film Nicholas and Alexandra.

Now in his seventies he is still in demand particularly as a voiceover artist which has included his narration in the comedy series 'Little Britain'. In a 2005 survey of British adults his voice was voted the fourth most recognisable after the Queen, Margaret Thatcher and Tony Blair. In 1986 he moved to live in converted school in Maidstone with his third wife Sue before emigrating to France in 2002.

KEN DODD

Voted the most popular Merseysider in a poll, he is one of the nation's treasures. Ken Dodd, the Squire of Knotty Ash, is also one of the hardest working comics in show business.

Ken was born on 8 November 1927 at 76 Thomas Lane in Knotty Ash where he still lives. His grandparents had bought the house when they came from Wales to live in Liverpool. His grandmother was distinguished in becoming the city's first woman magistrate. Ken's father Arthur was a coal merchant delivering coal in the surrounding area, as did his elder brother Bill. A real family affair, it was his mothers Sarah's job to collect the money from Thursday to Saturday . Ken was educated at Knotty Ash Primary School and then the Holt High School on Queens Drive. When he was seven he came off his bicycle damaging his front teeth, which in later years became his trade mark and he was able to use this mishap to his advantage. He left school at 14 and for a while worked with his father delivering coal. He decided to branch out on his own and formed his own

48 Butler Jas. and
50 Johnson Thos., Jun., insur. a
54 Walsh Louis
56 Pattenden Percy
   Knotty Ash County Pri
   (Infants') School
68 Beattie Jas., Jun., bldr
70 Edwards Arth
72 Warbrick Mrs. Emma Jane
74 Martin Miss Lucy
76 Dodd Arth. coal dlr
140 Gunning Herbt. Edwd
142 McCormick Jn
144 Butterworth Jsph. Fredk
146 Phillips Eric

Eilia

148 Swarbrick Mrs. Clarinda
150 Lowe Arth., Jun
152 Price Eric Geo
152A Hartley Mrs. Mary
154 Atherton Thos. V

Thov

THOMAS LANE

business Kaydee Products selling items such as bleach and firelighters to homes in the Dovecot, West Derby and Huyton districts. Music ran in Ken's family, his father was an accomplished saxophonist and his mother an equally proficient pianist. Ken was a member of the choir at his Parish church, St John's Knotty Ash where he still worships. He commenced performing while at primary school presenting Punch and Judy shows and was eight years of age when he did his first ventriloquist act at St Edward's Orphanage close to his home at Thingwall Hall in Thomas Lane on Christmas Day 1935. After learning the trade at various local venues Ken made his professional debut at the Nottingham Empire in 1954. He has now completed over 50 years in show business and is possibly the last exponent of the great British Music Hall tradition. He is also an accomplished singer having had four UK top ten hits including a number one with 'Tears' in 1965. In December 2007 he had a hernia operation which caused him to cancel several of his legendary shows but was back on stage within a month and despite being an octogenarian he continues to work as hard as ever and is still much in demand. He presented The History of Liverpool Comedians at St George's Hall in April 2008. A bronze statue of Ken commissioned by Merseytravel was unveiled at Lime Street Station in 2008. The statue was designed by Liverpool based artist Tom Murphy and depicts Ken with the late Labour MP Bessie Braddock.

What a day missus! Ken Dodd meets his fans (left).
Opposite : The face that launched a thousand quips
Doddy is also one of ~Liverpool's most successful
recording stars.

LITA ROZA

The first Scouser to have a number one hit. with How Much is That Doggie in the Window? Lita Roza was truly versatile.

Lillian Patricia Lita Roza was born on 14 March 1926, the eldest of seven children, her parents were both in show business. Her father Francis had previously worked at ICI in Speke and then as a marine engineer. Her mother Elizabeth had been a dancer. Lita's grandmother's name was Delacruz being of Spanish descent. The family lived at 13 Upper Pitt Street a narrow house on four floors, next to Morgans Stables. Lita attended the nearby St Michael's school in Cornwallis Street. Also living in Upper Pitt street at number 28 was George Jamieson who became April Ashley, at the time the most famous and publicised transsexual in Britain who later moved to 51 Teynham Crescent in Norris Green. Lita was a good swimmer and used Cornwallis Street baths most days. She won the Liverpool Shipwreck and Humane Society silver medal, and the district diving championship when just eleven. The family moved to 92 Wordsworth Street off Lodge Lane and Lita attended St Michael's school in Frederick Street and then went on to Granby Street Secondary Modern. After leaving school she was employed firstly at a florists in Lodge Lane and then at Pollock's pram shop at 11 Renshaw Street. She then worked at the Home and Colonial Store, 108 Lodge Lane where she was well known for giving extra rations to customers or deliberately cracking a few eggs so that they would have an egg for the weekends ! Lita was so good at patting butter that she was sent to other branches to show the staff how to do it. She had by now embarked on her show business career and her big break came when she sang with Harry Roy – the bandleader at the Coventry Hippodrome. Lita is best known for being the first artist from Liverpool and the first British female singer to have a UK number one hit, with the novelty record ' How Much Is That Doggie In The Window ' ? in 1953. She hated the song and rarely sang it again. She also sang with Ted Heath's band. In later years she enjoyed her retirement in the London area and rarely made public appearances although in 2001 she presided at the inauguration of the Liverpool Wall of Fame in Mathew Street.

She made her last public appearance at BBC Radio Merseyside in November 2002. Lita a remarkable lady died August 2008.

Lita in the studio in the 50's

In 1927/28 Dixie Dean scored an amazing 60 league goals for Everton in just 39 games – a record that is never likely to be beaten.

Willam Ralph Dean was born 22 January 1907 and lived at 313 Laird Street in the north end of Birkenhead.

There were six children in the family and Dixie was the only boy.

His father also William worked as a railwayman for Great Western Railways, and later as a fried fish dealer. Dixie attended Laird Street Council School leaving at the age of 13 and joining his father on the railways.

His nickname was Digsy as when he was playing tag, a popular children's game of the time with other children he had a habit of digging the other children in the back. From an early age he had a passion for football and would spend hours throwing a ball onto a roof and as it dropped meet it with his head.

He played for the school team and later for the railways side. His last amateur club was Pensby Institute and it was there that he would become known as Dixie. He signed for Tranmere Rovers in 1925 for £3,000 scoring 32 goals in his first season.

The following year he was involved in a serious motor cycle accident when it was feared he would not play again but he recovered and joined Everton for whom he would play 433 games and score 383 goals.

He also scored 18 goals for England in just 16 appearances.

In season 1927/28 he scored an amazing 60 league goals for Everton in just 39 games a record that is never likely to be beaten. On retiring from football he became the landlord of the Dublin Packet Public House in Chester before returning to Birkenhead in 1961 to work for Littlewoods Pools in Canning Street in the town. His latter days saw his health deteriorate and his right leg was amputated in 1976 - a cruel twist of fate.

He lived with his daughter Barbara who cared for him until his death on 1 March 1980.

Ironically he died at his beloved Goodison Park following a derby match against Liverpool. Barbara had taken him to the game and had arranged to pick him up afterwards. As if he had a premonition of his death his last words to Barbara was to thank her for all she had done for him. When she arrived at the ground at 5pm she was given the sad news.

In 2001 a statue to his memory was unveiled by his son who is also called William Ralph Dean but known as Geoff. It bore the words, Footballer, Gentleman, Evertonian'. There is also a street Deansway named after him in Birkenhead.

A true great, which begs the question, what would his value be today ?

Record making Dixie Dean leading out his beloved Blues (left) Hot shot on target at Goodsion. Below : One of the bests headers of the ball - muti talented Dixie.

DIXIE DEAN

IAN BROUDIE

A singer-songwriter, performer and producer, Ian Broudie has a gift for melody and heart-felt lyrics and a sense of humour to match. A shining light in Liverpool's rich music scene.

The family lived at 28 Menlove Gardens North not far from John Lennon's home in Menlove Avenue.

Ian Broudie was born on 4 August 1958 into a Jewish family, the second youngest of four children to Dennis a businessman and Reneee.

It was Robert his eldest brother who first introduced him to the guitar.

Robert would go on to become one of the city's leading solicitors with his own firm R M Broudie and Co in Dale Street. Tragically he died. Ian's other brother, David is a retired businessman.

It was Eric's club in Mathew Street that Ian says shaped him as a musician and also as a human being.

He was a product of the eighties when unemployment was high and Liverpool experienced its fair share of social problems.

Ironically, though, Ian feels that this sparked creativity in the city and was a period when many outstanding bands emerged.

He is of course best known for his work as leader of the Lightning Seeds and his co-writing 'Three Lions', England's Euro 1996 anthem.

A prolific songwriter and producer his production credits include local bands the Bunnymen, Ian McNabb's Icicle Works and latterly The Coral and The Zutons.

Music is his first love but a close second are Liverpool Football Club and his earliest memory is of attending Anfield in the sixties and being fascinated by the grown men around him singing their various songs which no doubt included 'You'll Never Walk Alone'.

His favourite band is the Beatles whose records would be played by his elder brothers when Ian was growing up, and whom he saw at the Empire Theatre in Lime Street in 1965 as a seven-year-old.

He says he was later drawn as if by ancestral voices to Mathew Street at the age of sixteen by which time he was already an accomplished guitarist.

His favourite composition is 'The Life of Riley' which is named after Riley – his son.

The Lightning Seeds with frontman Ian sporting his trademark shades (above) and solo (opposite).

MENLOVE GARDENS NORTH

Nelson Saml
Newman Wm
Henry David Graham, M.B
Gwyther Rev. Cyril E
20 Rubin Phillip
22 Tyler Ja. B
24 Pugh Mrs. Alice
26 Harris Sydney
28 Broudie Dennis
30 Thomas Miss Margt. Elunc
    Ch.B. physcn. and surgn
32 Atkinson-Blaxland Rupert
              Menlove garden

MENLOVE GARDENS

Ian Broudie one of the shining stars of the Liverpool music scene.

RINGO STARR

Enjoying a post show moment during Beatle-mania (left).

Ringo Starr was the lad made good from Dingle. The most working class of the Fab Four, he dedicated his album Liverpool 8 to his home town.

Richard Starkey, an only child, was born on 7 July 1940 at 9 Madryn Street, Liverpool 8. At the time of writing this house is still standing but there is constant speculation as to its future. When he was just three years old his parents, Richard and Elsie, split up. His mother stayed at Madryn Street for a short while before moving the short distance with young Richard, to 10 Admiral Grove a small two-up and two-down terraced house. This would be Ringo's home until 1963. To make ends meet Elsie worked as a barmaid at the nearby Empress Pub. The Empress is featured on Ringo's first solo album 'Sentimental Journey'. Richie, as he was always known to his friends, would spend a lot of time with Grandma and Grandad Starkey who lived at 59 Madryn Street. He was educated firstly at St Silas Church of England Primary School in Pengwern Street and then at Dingle Vale Secondary Modern (now Shorefields) in Dingle Vale. Ronnie Wycherly (Billy Fury) and Billy Hatton later of the Fourmost also attended St Silas at the same time as Richie. However like Billy Fury, his education was hindered because of ill health and he consequently missed a considerable amount of schooling. He spent almost two years in hospital firstly at Myrtle Street and then Heswall Childrens' Hospital. When he left school at 15 he had a succession of jobs which included British Rail messenger boy, a steward on the cruise boat 'St Tudno' that sailed between Liverpool and Llandudno and as an apprentice joiner at Henry Hunt and Son Ltd in Woodend Avenue, Hunts Cross. Ringo's mother remarried in April 1954, a Londoner called Harry Graves, whom Ringo took to straight away. In 1961 he celebrated his 21st Birthday with a party at 10 Admiral Grove with 80 people cramming into the tiny house. The guests included Cilla Black ,Gerry Marsden and Rory Storm. Ringo was the drummer with Rory Storm and the Hurricanes at this time. This was the band he was with before joining the Beatles. Elsie and Harry stayed in their home until 1965 when Ringo bought them a luxurious bungalow at 10 Heath Hey in Woolton where they spent their remaining years. Ringo returned to Liverpool in 2008 as part of the City of Culture celebrations and performed at St George's Hall.

During his stay he spoke fondly of his upbringing in the Dingle in an exclusive interview with the Liverpool Echo.

ADMIRAL GROVE (8).
Park street.
RIGHT SIDE.

1 Johnson Mrs. H
2 Stokes Chas
3 Conroy Danl
4 Muir Wm
5 Doyle Mrs. C
6 Gill Clement
7 Hewitt Mrs. Marion
8 Hutchinson Rt
9 Povey Stanley
10 Graves Harry
11 Myles Edwd. Jsph
12 Daley Wm
13 Pickston Mrs. Agnes
15 Dutton Jas
16 Dudley Michl

Ringo Starr, aka Richard Starkey, came back for the launch of the Capital of Culture in 2008 and to announce his album – Liverpool 8.

He went on a private tour of his old school along with wife Barbara Bach. He showed her the area that shaped him when he was a poorly child in and out of hospital.

The places that appeared on Beatle TV footage when Beatlemania hit here also visited.

A pst revisted to Madryn Street and then further up and over the road in Admiral Grove.

Ringo, who now lives in America and Monaco, is nos stranger to controversy and upset proud Scousers on a TV chat show when asked what he missed about Liverpool.

He said 'nothing.'

A joke,surely? Was this, as many believe, simply irreverent humour? Because Ringo did name his single and album after the area he was born in.

Ringo is still well respected in Dingle – notably in the atmospheric Empress pub.Inside there is a 'Starr shrine.' Ringo featured the pub on the album cover of the Sentimental Journey album.

On the daily Magical Mystery Tours visitors from all over the world are amazed at the tough working class area that the drummer was brought up in.

Madryn Street was actually condemned for demolishment and many have suggested that it be built brick-by-brick in a museum. When Ringo heard he laughed:"But I wasn't born in a museum."

Ringo really did show his true colours when he told Peter Grant of the Liverpool Echo that 'Liverpool is in my soul'. "I am still on sentimental journey."

And all joking aside,Liverpool should celebrate the fab fact that from the streets of Dingle a true-working class hero was born.

Ringo on the set of Help! with actress Eleanor Bron and (right) meeting the Maharishi.

Jimmy McGovern another of the city's teachers turned award-winning writer.

Born in 1949 in the Everton area of the city, Jimmy is the fifth of nine children to Jane and Bill McGovern. The family lived at 45 Greenside off Brunswick Road.

He attended a Catholic Primary and then St Francis Xavier School in Shaw Street.

At an early age he developed a stammer something which has never left him.

He left school with six passes at GCE O'Level.

Whilst having a respect for the church he is critical of his Catholic education and his experience of being taught by the Jesuits.

He is critical too of corporal punishment which has undoubtedly influenced his career as a writer.

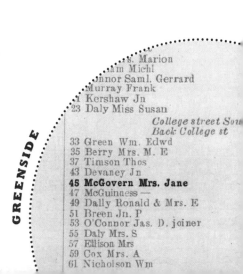

GREENSIDE

s. Marion
ia'm Michl
nnor Saml. Gerrard
Murray Frank
1 Kershaw Jn
23 Daly Miss Susan

College street Sou
Back College st

33 Green Wm. Edwd
35 Berry Mrs. M. E
37 Timson Thos
43 Devaney Jn
45 McGovern Mrs. Jane
47 McGuinness —
49 Dally Ronald & Mrs. E
51 Breen Jn. P
53 O'Connor Jas. D. joiner
55 Daly Mrs. S
57 Ellison Mrs
59 Cox Mrs. A
61 Nicholson Wm

After a series of dead end jobs which included working at Butlins as a waiter and in a car factory he attended a writers' school and then taught English at Quarry Bank, John Lennon's old school and now Calderstones Comprehensive.

He became a full-time writer in 1982 and wrote scripts for Brookside particularly about the character Bobby Grant played by Ricky Tomlinson.

A strong friendship with Ricky was forged which remains to this day.

In 1983 Jimmy wrote the play 'City Echoes' which is loosely based on his own experiences of growing up in Greenside.

The play was premiered at the Playhouse and dealt with the life and hard times of a working class Liverpool family struggling to cope in the post war years. He has since gone on to write several award-winning dramas each with a hard-hitting social message including Hillsborough, Cracker, Bloody Sunday and Dockers.

Jimmy has a special affinity with the Liverpool Dockers and is a frequent visitor to the Casa Club in Hope Street, which was originally purchased by a group of dock workers.

He is also extremely loyal to his family and most Friday evenings can be found in a favourite pub playing cards and dominoes with his brothers and other family members. He lives in Gateacre with his wife Eileen to whom he has three children, Nicky 36, Joanne 35 and Jimmy 34.

He is also a grandfather of four.

His critically acclaimed musical stage play King Cotton was a key part of the Liverpool European Capital of Culture 2008.

Jimmy during the screening of the award winning drama Hillsborough (left) On this page, Jimmy relaxing after appearing at the Writing On the Wall festival encouragng new writers.

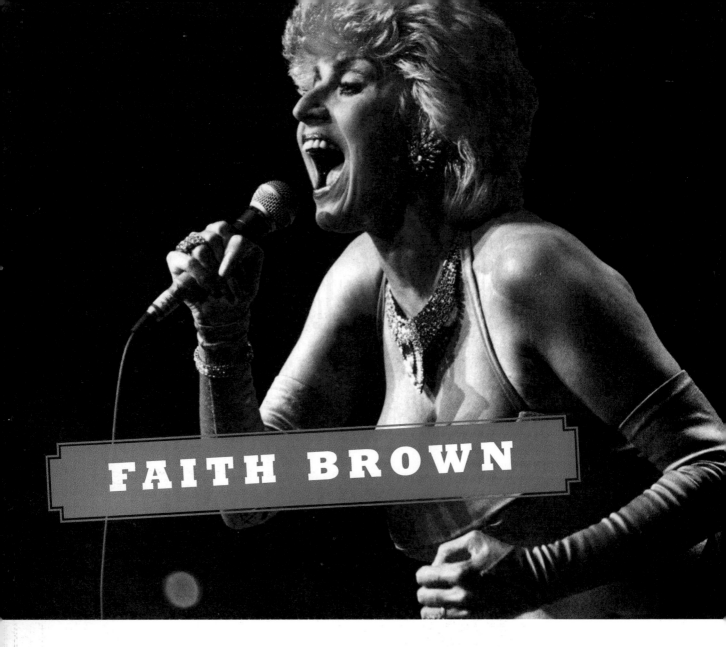

FAITH BROWN

Faith Brown has a CV that is the envy of many female performers. Pop singer, comic, chat show host and West End superstar.

Born Irene Carroll on 28 May 1944 the only girl in a family of five children who lived at 12 Olney Street off County Road, Walton.

She attended St Francis De Sales School in Hale Road, Walton where she was known by the nickname 'Iceberg Carroll'.

She made a name for herself at school for doing impressions of Sister Gertrude one of the teachers.

When she left school she worked at Lewis's store in Ranelagh Street for eighteen months doing oven cleaning demonstrations and selling china. She was also appearing with three of her brothers Lee, Ron and Mike in a singing group The Carrolls who achieved a reasonable degree of success on the cabaret scene and who also made several Television appearances which included the 'The David Frost Show'.

They released a single 'Surrender Your Love' which made the Radio Caroline charts but did not succeed nationally. The band stayed together for five years before Irene decided to go solo which coincided with her change of name to Faith Brown.

Her big break came at The Orrell Park Ballroom when whilst singing her skirt split, and she was so embarrassed that she broke into an impression of TV star Hylda Baker.This so impressed an agent Byron Godfey who was in the audience that she was signed up after the show. She had met her musician husband Len Wadey when singing at the Rialto Ballroom when she was just sixteen, he being twelve years her senior.He proposed at Reeces' Restaurant in Parker Street.

The couple married at St Francis De Sales Church on 8 September 1966 just a few weeks after her mother died at just 46 years of age. The wedding reception was held at the Melody Inn Club in Wallasey Village attended by about 50 guests.

They have one daughter Danielle born in 1978. Faith is regarded as one of the leading impressionists and her impression of the former Prime Minister Margaret Thatcher is still appreciated particularly in the U.S.A and has won her international acclaim. She has appeared in the late TV soap Brookside playing the role of Anne Bradley and has also starred in the Faith Brown Chat Show.

She currently lives with her family in Buckinghamshire.

Oh Carroll... Faith Brown the chameleon of show business (above).
On stage belting out a rock number. (opposite)

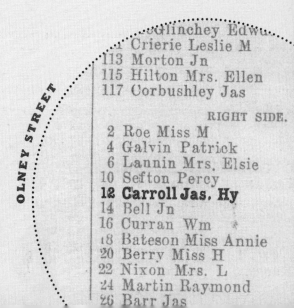

McGlinchey Edwd
Crierie Leslie M
113 Morton Jn
115 Hilton Mrs. Ellen
117 Corbushley Jas

RIGHT SIDE.

2 Roe Miss M
4 Galvin Patrick
6 Lannin Mrs. Elsie
10 Sefton Percy
12 **Carroll Jas. Hy**
14 Bell Jn
16 Curran Wm
18 Bateson Miss Annie
20 Berry Miss H
22 Nixon Mrs. L
24 Martin Raymond
26 Barr Jas

OLNEY STREET

ROGER McGOUGH

Roger McGough is a juggler of words.
Poet, singer with pop band Scaffold and a
Beatles screenwriter. A multi-skilled Scouser.

Born in 1937 in Ruthven Road, Seaforth, the road was demolished in the early 1970's to make way for a flyover called Princes Way.

Roger is the eldest of two children to Roger and Mary McGough. His father worked on the docks and died at just 53 years of age. During the Second World War Roger was evacuated with his younger sister Brenda to Chirk in Wales. He was educated firstly at the Star of the Sea Primary school in Seaforth before passing the scholarship to St Mary's Catholic College in Crosby where he was taught by the Christian Brothers. He was a class mate of John Askew who later changed his name to Johnny Gentle, and who toured with the Silver Beatles in Scotland in 1960. Roger left St Mary's in 1954 with three passes at GCE A Level and studied at Hull University where he developed an interest in poetry.

The works of Phillip Larkin particularly inspired him. During vacation periods he had several jobs in Liverpool including working in a toy and a bread factory and at Tate and Lyle sugar refinery in Love Lane close to the docks. He also spent a season as a holiday representative. On leaving University he commenced teaching at St Kevin's Comprehensive School in Kirkby before becoming a lecturer at Mabel Fletcher Technical College for Women in Picton Road, Wavertree. He would spend a lot of his spare time at the Philharmonic Hotel and at Streates Coffee Bar on Mount Pleasant where he mingled with the likes of Adrian Henri, Brian Patten, John Gorman, Mike McCartney and Arthur Dooley. He lived for a short time with Adrian Henri and Adrian's wife Joyce in a flat at 64 Canning Street, Liverpool 8. Roger was by now utterly immersed in the Liverpool Art Culture scene which eventually would see him abandoning his career in teaching. He can boast numerous achievements including a period in the hugely successful singing group Scaffold who had a number one single in the UK charts ' Lily The Pink' and several other hits and he has written over 50 poetry books for which he has won several awards. He was responsible for much of the humorous dialogue in the Beatles' animated film Yellow Submarine, although he did not receive an on screen credit. He received the Freedom of the City in 2001 and the CBE in 2005. He currently presents Poetry Please on BBC Radio 4 and lives in London but makes many visists to Liverpool theatres to perform.

This elephant will never forget Roger's rhymes (opposite).
(left) The poet in the 60s

RUTHVEN ROAD

...s. Bessie

Vivian

UTHVEN ROAD, LITHERLAND (2
89 *Bridge road.*
LEFT SIDE.
1 Perks Mrs. Edith
3 Nichols Jas. Edwd. labourer
5 Haslam Jas. Hy
7 Carte Sydney Jas. seaman
9 Sefton Thos. E
11 **McGough Roger**
13 Thomas Mrs. Grace
15 McGrath Mrs. Julia
17 Roberts Norman Victor
19 Savage Fras. gasman
21 Butler Miss Elsie
23 Ainsworth Fredk. Geo. labourer
25 Cantrell Edwd

Hope Street has a cathedral at either end and is home to the Everyman Theatre. A living, breathing thoroughfare and cultural centre for famous pubs and top class restaurants.

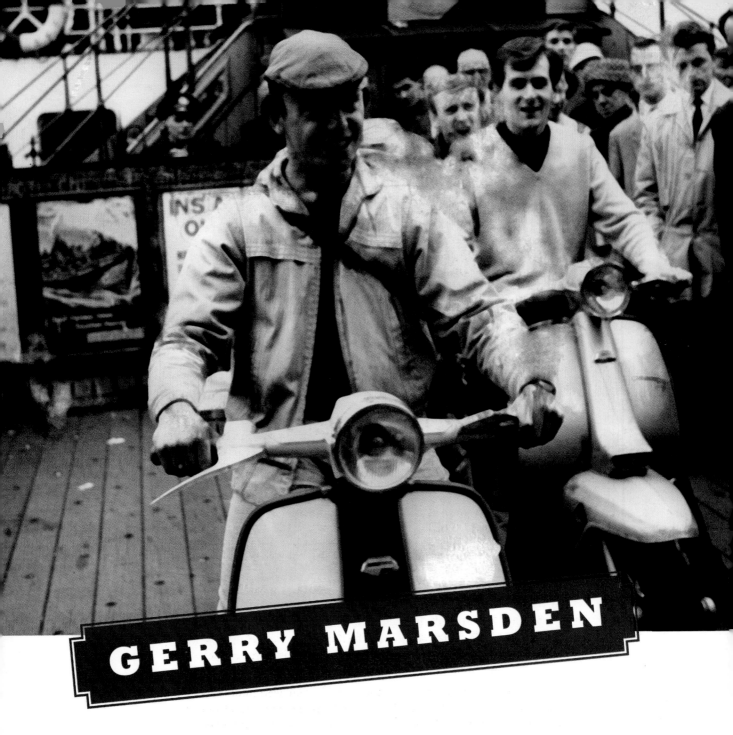

GERRY MARSDEN

**Another of the Dingle Dynamos.
Gerry Marsden, singer-songwriter, still tours
the world with his classic songs and pure
Scouse sense of humour. His catchphrase is
Get In there. He always does!**

Born Gerard Marsden on 24 September 1942 the family home was at 8 Menzies Street in the Dingle.

His father Fred worked on the railways and played the ukulele in his spare time. His mother Mary had two jobs: school cleaner and she also served in the local fish and chip shop.

Gerry attended Our Lady of Mount Carmel School in South Hill Road, Dingle and as a youngster was quite a promising boxer being a member of the Florence Institute in Mill Street. Music though was his first love and when his father bought him a guitar he formed his own skiffle group which included Brian O'Hara who was to become a member of the Fourmost.

They played at the Labour Club in Peel Street and also at the Florence Institute. On leaving school he had several jobs including helping with coal deliveries, a chest maker, Woolworths store in Church Street on van deliveries and at the Kardomah Tea Factory in Redcross Street.

He changed the name of his group to The Mars Bars and in 1959 they became a rock and roll band.

With brother Fred now in the line up he hit on the name Pacemakers which has remained to this day although Gerry is the only original member. Freddie Marsden who had run The Pacemaker Driving School died in December 2006. Signed by Brian Epstein Gerry and the Pacemakers managed to achieve something even the Beatles could not emulate, their first three singles reaching number one in the charts. It would be over twenty years until Frankie Goes To Hollywood another band from Liverpool managed a similar feat.

He married Pauline who was from the Hunts Cross area on 11 October 1965 at St Mary's Church in Woolton .

A daughter Yvette was born in Clatterbridge Hospital on 30 October 1966 followed by Vicky in 1980. By now the Marsdens were living in Croft Drive East in Caldy. His two most famous songs are undoubtedly ' You'll Never Walk Alone ' adopted by the Kop at Liverpool FC in 1964 and still sung today and ' Ferry 'cross the Mersey ' which is played several times daily on the Mersey Ferries.

An irrepressible character Gerry bounced back from heart trouble and continues to perform on a regular basis both in this country and abroad. He has always lived on Merseyside and is a great champion of the region.

caption (Opposite)

Gerry on location in the film 'Ferry Cross the Mersey.

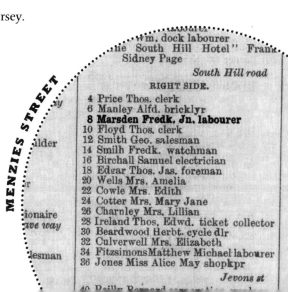

THE REAL THING

Chris and Eddie Amoo, singer-songwriter are home-grown stars in the Real Thing. The much-loved band are multi-hit makers who are still touring and enjoying sell out tours.

If the Cavern Club played a significant role in the development of the Beatles and the other Merseybeat bands of the time, there is no doubt that Stanley House (see below) situated at 130 Upper Parliament Street, was a key venue in the origins of many of the black bands from Liverpool 8.

Stanley House was a social meeting place where young met old, black met white and people would enjoy the many facilities on offer including dancing football and snooker. The Chants previously called The Shades made their first public performance here in 1962. The band all from Liverpool 8 comprised Joe and Edmund Ankrah, Nat Smeda, Alan Harding and Eddie Amoo.

Joe and Edmunds father was a minister at the African Churches Mission Church and a fine singer, and he taught his sons how to harmonise.

So indebted were they to Stanley House that Eddie Amoo in 1964 wrote 'One Star' as a tribute to the social centre. Despite enormous popularity and some strong single releases on Pye and other labels somehow chart success eluded The Chants.

For a brief period Brian Epstein was their manager but even this failed to give them the break through they deserved.

However not many bands can claim to be backed by the Beatles, for when they turned up at the Cavern for an audition without a backing group the Beatles offered to back them despite Brian Epstein's objections which were overruled by John Lennon. They disbanded in 1975 with Joe and Edmund joining a group called Ashanti and Eddie Amoo with his brother Chris joining a soul group, The Real Thing. Other members of The Real Thing were Ray Lake, Kenny Davis and Dave Smith.

In 1976 UK chart success was finally achieved when 'You To Me Are Everything' reached number one. This was followed by a further four top twenty hits.

From time to time the band has included other members and with three of the founder members still on board they continue to perform. Eddie was born 5 May 1950 and Chris 11 October 1952 to their mother Moya and father Robert Amoo who was from Ghana and a proficient guitarist. Away from music Chris Amoo is a regular on the dog breeding circuit and in 1987 his dog Grant was crowned the supreme champion at Crufts.

Eddie's four daughters have kept up the family's musical tradition by forming their own band which Eddie has managed.

The Real Thing that was then (opposite) this is now (left)

JOHN PEEL

Peelie was the mentor for so many of today's bands. A radio DJ, he later became a TV star and witty columnist. He was also an LFC fan.

Born John Robert Parker Ravenscroft at Heswall Cottage Hospital in 1939 just days before the outbreak of World War Two, John was the eldest of three boys. The Cottage Hospital is now a private home. The family residence was at Haddon Corner, Neston Road, Burton, Wirral and for the first six years of John's life he did not see his father who was away fighting for King and Country. John was educated firstly at Westbourne School, Wood lane, Neston and for a brief period at Woodlands School in Deganwy. At the age of eleven he went to the exclusive Shrewsbury Public School and whilst there established his first link with the City of Liverpool. The school had an arrangement with Shrewsbury House Boys Club in Portland Place, Everton, whereby pupils would visit the school ostensibly to help the inner city youngsters. However John would later state that he learnt a great deal from his experience at the club and related far better to the inner city lads than he did with the generally upper class boys at his own school. He particularly enjoyed playing 5 a side football at Shrewsbury House. His parents divorced when he was in his early teens and he was sent to live with his grandmother in Heswall. Before undertaking his National Service he worked for a short while as an office boy at Baumann Hinde and Co Ltd., Cotton Merchants who had offices at 4 Cotton Exchange, Old Hall Street, Liverpool. His father was a Cotton Merchant whose firm Strauss and Co., were based in the same building. A staunch supporter of Liverpool Football Club his daughter was christened Florence Victoria Shankly Ravenscroft whilst his sons had Anfield added to their names. He was working as a DJ in Dallas, Texas, when 'Beatlemania' hit the States and his Merseyside connections proved useful and indirectly, helped launch his road to success. A stalwart of Radio 1 since its inception in 1967 and more recently presenter of Radio 4's ' Home Truths ' John was a very private individual and committed family man. He died suddenly on holiday in Peru in 2004 and his wife Sheila still lives at Peel Acres in rural Suffolk, the home she shared with John for thirty-three years. A real broadcaster and one of life's genuine people. He is sorely missed.

John Peel –always in the hot seat (opposite)
A hit-maker plays the jukebox (right)

PETE McGOVERN

A troubador. Pete McCovern came up with a song that is close to all Scousers' hearts In My Liverpool Home.

The writer in 1961 of Liverpool's unofficial anthem " In My Liverpool Home " was born Peter John McGovern on 28 October 1927 the youngest of 14 children, in Regent Street off Great Howard Street, which as the song suggests was situated near the docks. The house was bombed in 1941 and Peter went to live with his sister in Hunts Cross. His father a docker enjoyed folk singing and as a young child Peter would sing along with him at family gatherings. He passed the scholarship and won a place to the prestigious St Edmund's College in Sandfield Park, West Derby but his parents could not afford to buy his sports kit and he was transferred to Queen Elizabeth School in Anfield. In 1950 he married Audrey McGann and the couple moved to London. Audrey was the inspiration behind Bridget McGann who features in " In My Liverpool Home " with the line 'When I grew up I met Bridget McGann'. In 1984 when Liverpool and Everton played each other for the first time in a major cup final Peter led the community singing before 100,000 fans changing the words to 'In my Merseyside home.' He had started work with British Rail starting as a wheel tapper before retiring in 1992 as safety manager. He moved back to Merseyside and the couple lived in Bromborough. He became secretary of the Merseyside Pensioners Association. A keen trade unionist throughout his working life he championed the cause for a better state pension and other benefits for pensioners. An accomplished writer and singer his contribution to the Merseyside folk scene is immeasurable and he was good friends with the Spinners who recorded " In My Liverpool Home " and sang it at most of their concerts, although only Hughie Jones was actually from the city. There is a seventy minute version of the song recorded at BBC Radio Merseyside at the instigation of Spencer Leigh, by the Spinners, Mike McCartney, Adria Henri and Sinbad the window cleaner in Brookside. Peter and Audrey had two children Maureen and Mike and five grandchildren. They enjoyed staying at their holiday home in Transfynedd in Gwynedd and it was here on 1 April 2006 that Peter passed away shortly after watching Liverpool's victory against West Bromwich Albion on television. He had celebrated the victory with a can of Guinness and had just completed his daily crossword when he went to bed and died in his sleep.

REGENT STREET

...opkeeper	
...ard labourer	37
...gham Christopher	39
...ne Joseph ship painter	41
...obin Mrs. Mary	43
...Quinn Patrick labourer	45
63 Moonan Thomas dock labourer	47
65 O'Reilly James dock labourer	49
67 Doherty Mrs. Catharine	51
69 O'Reilly Patrick labourer	53
RIGHT SIDE.	
2 Mitchell Patrick dock labourer	2
4 Larkin Charles coalheaver	6
6 Miley Miles labourer	8
8 McHugh Patrick dock labourer	10
10 Ward Nicholas dock labourer	12
12 Murphy Peter dock labourer	14
14 Byrne John " Marco Polo" P.H.	16
16 Moffitt Patrick watchman	18
18 McGovern Thomas dock labourer	20
20 Murphy William dock labourer	22
22 Slavin Mrs. Sarah	24
24 McVeigh Thomas dock labourer	26
26 Iddon Mrs. Margaret lodging house	28
28 Moane Miss Elizabeth dressmaker	30
30 McDonough Mrs. Ellen	32

IAN
TRACEY

Ian Tracey at work (opposite) in Liverpool and (left) pulling out the organ stops.

Recognised as one of the leading organists in the country Ian Tracey has frequently performed for the BBC and made many records for EMI and worked with Sir Paul McCartney.

Ian was born at the Elmswood Nursing Home in Mossley Hill and the family lived at 12 Liddell Road in West Derby.

Organist at Liverpool's Anglican Cathedral since 1980, Ian was born on 27 May 1955.

His Scottish father William was a watchmaker and jeweller whilst his mother Helene, who was from Merseyside, was a social worker.

They then moved to 38 Corinthian Avenue off Derby Lane, Old Swan and Ian attended Corinthian Avenue Primary School from 1960 to 1966. Subsequently he lived at 67 Beauclair Drive off Woolton Road and at 55 Rodney Street.

On leaving primary school he attended Highfield School in Old Swan before undertaking two years of study at Trinity College, London.

A short period of study was then spent in France and then a year at St Katherine's College in Woolton.

A professional musician from the commencement of his working career, Ian was director of music at St Edmund's College, Devonshire Road from 1976 to 1982 and lecturer in music at C.F. Mott College in Prescot until 1988.

In 1983 he was the first organist from Liverpool to play at the service of remembrance at the Royal Albert Hall. Recognised as one of the leading organists in the country he has frequently performed for the BBC and made many records for EMI.

He is also consultant organist at St George's Hall and chorus master at the Royal Liverpool Philharmonic Orchestra.

His achievements are considerable and have been recognised by numerous awards which include Professor, Fellow and Organist at Liverpool John Moores University.

In October 2007 he assumed the title of 'Organist Titulaire' at The Cathedral, which whilst assuring his continued involvement gives him more time to be involved in concerts, recitals, writing and lecturing.

CORINTHIAN AVENUE

joiner
Derek B
Mrs. Margt

Doric rd

Turnbull Harold W
24 Foote Geo
26 Little Mrs. Sarah
28 Mills Geo
30 Smith Mrs. A
32 Meehan Geo
34 Bulfield Geo
36 Thomas Leslie   IAN
38 Tracey Wm
40 Keating Wm
42 Keegan Mrs. Annie
44 Middlebrough Mrs. Edith

Abacus rd

LEFT SIDE
1 Cuddy Miss E. R

KEITH
CHEGWIN

Keith Chegwin has grown up in front of our eyes on his own TV shows such as Saturday Superstore, Breakfast TV and Extras.

Keith and his identical twin brother Jeffrey were born at Walton Hospital on 17 January 1957. The family home was at 37 Aintree Road and his father worked at a firm of Timber Merchants, his mother at a local shoe shop. He attended St George of England Secondary Modern School in Fernhill Road, Bootle where he was known as something of a prankster much to the exasperation of the teachers. From an early age encouraged by his parents he would put on shows at home for the local children and it was clear even at this stage that he possessed a natural talent for entertaining. With brother Jeff and his sister Janice he formed the Chegwins and they had their first booking at the Floral Pavilion in New Brighton in 1968 when Keith was only eleven. This was the start of a burgeoning career in show business for this multi-faceted performer known as Cheggers, with perhaps his best work being in youth oprogrammes such as 'Swap Shop'. His sister Janice Long is the well known Radio One DJ and one time 'Top of the Pops ' presenter. She was also for a number of years a presenter at Radio Merseyside.

Keith suffered from a serious addiction to alcohol for a number of years and his career waned for a while. The pressures of over working began to take their toll and Keith would take refuge in the bottle. The problem became so serious that he spent some time at the Priory Clinic. He courageously decided to go public with regard to his problem giving interviews to the tabloids and also TV including the Richard and Judy show.

With great support from Alcoholics Anonymous the slow path to recovery was commenced and his career was back on track again. He wrote a book " Shaken But Not Stirred "about his personal problems. . He was married for a number of years to Maggie Philbin the couple divorcing in 1989.

They have a daughter Rose born in 1988. Keith married for a second time in 2000 to his long term partner Maria Fielden . They live in Berkshire with their son Ted born in 1998, where Keith has his own recording studio and does his own voiceovers from home.

In 2007 Keith won the BAFTA Childrens' award and can still be heard regularly on radio.

Kids' TV favourite Keith in the 80s (opposite).
Above with first wife Maggie Philbin (above)
Star of quiz Cheggers Plays Pop (above).

41

ALEXEI SAYLE

Alexei Sayle, comedian actor,
author and TV presenter. His
aggressive stage act belies hs
own softly-spoken nature.
A supporter and yet also
a critic of his home town
he has a loyal following.

Born on 7 August 1952, Alexei was the son of Joseph a railway guard from the Isle of Man and Malka who worked as a clerk at Littlewoods Pools.

The family home was at 5 Valley Road in Anfield not far from Liverpool FC's Stadium

His grandparents had emigrated from Russia.

Alecei's working class Jewish parents were members of the Communist Party of Great Britain (Marxist Leninist) which Alexei himself joined in 1968 when aged sixteen.

He describes himself as being of Lithuanian Jewish extraction.

Alexei attended Anfield Road Primary School and on passing the scholarship Alsop Grammar on Queens Drive.

Musicians Pete Wylie and Ian McCulloch were fellow pupils although a few years after Alexei.

This was followed by spells at Southport College of Art and Chelsea School of Art until 1974.

Prior to gaining a foothold in the media he worked as a DHSS clerk, on building sites, cleaner, dishwashing in hotels and as a part-time college lecturer. He also had spells at Southport College of Art and the Chelsea School of Art.

He married Linda Rawsthorne on the 1st January 1974 at Brougham Terrace Registrar's Office.

Linda lived at 30 Kingswood Dive in Crosby and her father Noel was a pipe-fitter.

Alexei's breakthrough came as a stand up comic at the Comedy Store in London and he has since developed a cult following.

A man of diverse talents he has enjoyed considerable success since the late 1970s with his own TV series, films and writing a number of books, as well as contributing to newspapers and magazines. He received excellent reviews for his comedy cameo in the film, 'Supergrass'.

In 1999 he appeared in the film' Swing' with fellow Liverpudlian Rita Tushingham.

In 2003 he made some rather derogatory comments about his home city which he quickly regretted saying that they were taken out of context. He apologised on the front page of the Liverpool Echo. In June 2008 he presented a three-part history of Liverpool broadcast on BBC 2 with favourable reviews. One of the first alternative comedians he once said " My contribution to the history of comedy is that I was the first comic who honestly does not care if the audience likes me or not ".

Sayling out on an aternative route (opposite);
Alexei still speaking his mind (above).

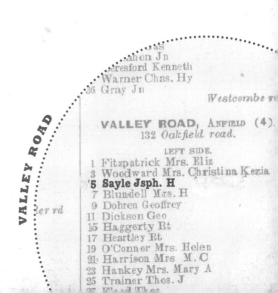

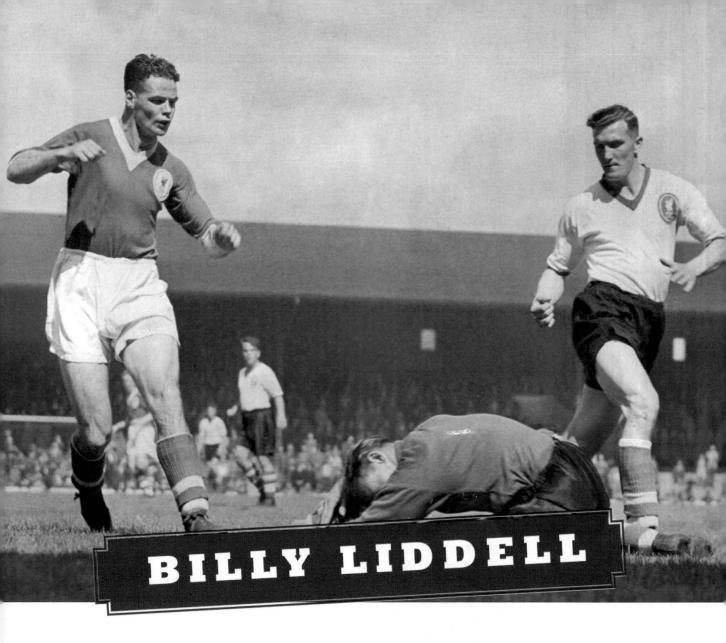

BILLY LIDDELL

Billy Liddell soccer superstar. Such was his fame and popularity on and off the pitch that his beloved club was often referred to as 'Liddlepool' and he was 'King Billy' to his many fans.

Born the son of a miner in Townhill near Dunfermline on 22 January 1922 William Beveridge Liddell was the eldest of six children. He was educated at Dunfermline High School before signing for Liverpool from Lochgelly Violets as a 16 year old amateur in June 1938. He lived in the city for half a century and for most of his playing days he resided at 2 Westfield Avenue in Huyton.

Further abodes included 23 Windsor Road in Roby and 31 Chequers Gardens, Liverpool 19.

His career was interrupted by the outbreak of the Second World War in 1939 and it was not until January 1946 that he made his official debut for the club.

He had served as a RAF navigator during the war. Billy made his final first team appearance for the reds in 1960 retiring the following year in a career that spanned 534 games and 228 goals.

He was twice selected to represent Great Britain against the Rest of the World.

Such was his contribution to the Liverpool team that it was referred to as 'Liddlepool' and he as 'King Billy' by the fans. An accountant by profession he worked for Simon Jude and West who had offices at 11 Victoria Street in the city centre, training two days a week at Melwood the clubs training ground. On his retirement from football he became a bursar at Liverpool University and was a Justice of the Peace for many years at the Liverpool Magistrates Court. He was also a Sunday School teacher at Court Hey Methodist Church in Roby.

A chivalrous loyal person he was always prepared to encourage youngsters in his role as a youth worker. A dedicated family man he and his wife Phyliss had twin boys Malcolm and David whom he would often watch playing for their 'life boys' team on Saturday mornings before setting out for Anfield.

He died from an alzheimers disease related illness which was first diagnosed in 1991, on 4 November 2001.

He spent his latter days in a nursing home in Mossley Hill.

In the present age of massive salaries paid to Premiership players it is remarkable even allowing for inflation that the highest wage paid to Billy in his career was £20 and for the greater part considerably less. Arguably the finest player to have represented the club a plaque to his memory was unveiled at Anfield on 4 November 2004 by his widow Phyliss and Ian Callaghan another ex Anfield legend .

Billy Liddell pride of Liverpool at Anfield (opposite);
Brian Hall has a quiet word in the ear of the great
Billy Liddell (above).

Paul McCartney and John Lennon turned an ordinary suburban place into an extraordinary world famous location.

PENNY LANE

One of the most photgraphed signs in the world along with Carnaby Street. This signpost, embedded into the ground to stop anyone running off with it, is near the Penny Lane Wine Bar and around the corner from St Barnabas Church where Paul McCartney was a choirboy.

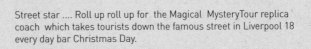

Clean up time - a law firm, based in Penny Lane, smartens up one of the famous street signs.

Those were the days. ... a Liverpool tram before the likes of schoolboys John, Paul and George would get a corporation bus from the famous roundabout where a pretty nurse would sell poppies from a tray.

Street star .... Roll up roll up for the Magical MysteryTour replica coach which takes tourists down the famous street in Liverpool 18 every day bar Christmas Day.

ADRIAN BOULT

A Boult from the blue. He was a child prodigy who attended his first public concert in 1895 at The Philharmonic Hall... when he was just six years of age.

Adrian Cedric Boult was the second and youngest child born to Cedric and Katherine in Chester on 8 April 1889, and spent the first two years of his life at 4 Abbots Hayes, Liverpool Road.

In 1891 the family moved to Brooke House,Blundellsands. His mother was a promising pianist whose career was thwarted by illness but she exposed Adrian to music beginning in infancy. His father was an oil merchant employed at F.J. Dodd and Co who had offices in Liverpool at 5 Tithebarn Street.

His work involved shipping Valvoline Oil and he travelled to the city centre by train from Blundellsands each day. In 1904 the family moved again, this time to Grange Road, West Kirby on the Wirral.

At the outbreak of the first World War, Adrian served his country by drilling the 16th battalion of the King's Liverpool Regiment firstly in West Kirby and then at Kimmel Park near St Asaph in North Wales He also worked as a translator for MI5.

A child prodigy he attended his first public concert in 1895 at the Philharmonic Hall when just six years of age. He had startled his parents by picking out tunes on the piano at just 18 months.

He attended the Dame School in Blundellsands before being transferred to Westminster Boarding School in London returning to West Kirby in the school holidays.

On 27 October 1914 he conducted an orchestra at the Public Hall in West Kirby which was such a success that he was asked to undertake a series of concerts in Liverpool including one at Sun Hall in Kensington which attracted 4,000 people.

Further concerts were held at the David Lewis Theatre in Great George Place. In 1922 his father retired through ill health and the family moved to Salisbury. Adrian a bald, austere moustached figure was now well known in concert halls up and down the country. He was the first director of the BBC Symphony Orchestra in 1930 and became their principal conductor.

He was made a companion of honour in the New Years Honours list of 1969. Adrian continued conducting until the age of 91 and died peacefully at a London nursing home on 22 February 1983.

There was no funeral because he had donated his body to medical research.

ELDER GROVE.
...isty Andrew boot maker
...mith Mrs. Elizabeth
Smith Harry carpet cleaner

Nairn John Gordon commercia...
Brookfield
84 Thomas Ifan horticulturist
Welsh Chapel
86 Moss Miss Annie "Brookfield"
Carpenters ...
Bell Miss Frances "Greenfield...
Boult Cedric R., J.P. merchant
"The Abbey Manor"
Ferguson John gardener
"The Abbey Manor Lodge...
Column re...

86 GRANGE ROAD

A pensive conductor before a concert (opposite); Sir Adrian Boult at rehearsal (above)

TOM O'CONNOR

13 SPENSER STREET

Geo. R. shipping c
iden Chas. Wm. railway

SPENSER STREET, Boot
115 Marsh lane.

LEFT SIDE.

7 Wardle Geo. Hy
9 Fagan Wm. Hy
11 Mawdsley Jn
13 O'Connor Patrick
15 Reynolds Ernest
17 Wedgwood Jsph
19 Stonehouse Wltr
21 Lynch Owen
23 Dickinson Albt
25 Flaherty Mrs. Sarah
27 Owens Nicholas
29 Garrigan Owen
33 Cain Thos. A., J.P. tra
official
35 Hearne Jas
37 Neilson —
39 Quinn Fras
41 Ferguson Edwd. motor dr

He is a natural comedian who took to the clubs and TV like a Scouse duck to the Mersey. He's an author, stand up and quiz show supremo.

Tom was born in the year that war broke out in 1939 on the 30th October. The family home was in Bootle at 13 Spenser Street. His father Pat worked nearby at Gladstone Docks as a quay foreman. Tom attended St Jame's Primary School in Chestnut Grove, Bootle and then St Mary's College a direct grammar school in Liverpool Road, Great Crosby. A fascination with films meant that he never missed the Saturday morning matinee at the Gainsborough Picture House in Knowsley Road , Bootle. He gained sufficient ' A ' Levels to be accepted for Simmaries Teachers Training College in Twickenham and it was here that he learned the guitar and also played drums in a skiffle group. A keen athlete he represented Lancashire at hurdling. He worked casually for a while on the docks no doubt gathering future material for gags. He also worked for a short time at the Liverpool Warehousing Company in Pall Mall. Following his marriage to Pat Finan on 28 July 1962 they set up home at 48 Hornby Road close to Walton Prison and his first teaching post was at ' St Joan Of Arc ' School in Peel Street, Bootle. Tom has said hat he owes teaching a lot for developing his comedy routine." The only way to get through to the kids was by telling gags " ! He had met Pat at a college ball he had organised in his position as college social secretary. With a young family and to gain additional income, he sang as part of a duo at the Selwyn Hotel , Selwyn Street, Anfield. He then branched out on his own as a comic and was soon playing popular venues such as Allisons in Litherland and the Wooky Hollow Club in Belmont Road. After 12 years as a teacher and attaining the position of deputy head he decided to pursue his entertainment career fulltime and got his big break in 1971 when he appeared on the popular TV series ' The Comedians '. His career blossomed and he is probably best known for game shows which included 'Name that Tune ' and ' Password. In 2006 he received an award for having appeared as a guest 100 times on the TV show 'Countdown'.

Now approaching his seventies he is still much in demand particularly as an after dinner speaker and a stalwart of the clubs and cruise liners.

Reflections of a top Scouse comic (opposite); Tom during a TV interview (below)

JOHN LENNON

Poet, Painter, wit - Beatle John was born to be great. In just forty years he became one of the most famous people on the planet.

John Winston Lennon was born on Wednesday 9 October 1940 at Oxford Street Maternity Hospital, Liverpool 7. He lived initially with his mother Julia and his grandparents Annie and George at 9 Newcastle Road, Wavertree not far from Penny Lane. His father a seafarer also lived there between voyages. When Julia's sister, Harriet offered Julia and John accommodation in her cottage at 120a Allerton Road in Woolton, Julia moved in with Harriet and her husband Norman. Johns Aunt Mimi (Mary Elizabeth) and her husband George lived in a fine semi detached house at 251 Menlove Avenue in Woolton and when problems developed between Johns parents he went to live with his aunt and uncle in 1945. In 1949 Julia now in a relationship with Bobby Dykins went to live at 1 Blomfield Road in Allerton. The couple had two girls Julia born 5 March 1947 and Jacqui born 26 October 1949. Mimi and George virtually became Johns surrogate parents and he was particularly close to George and was devastated when he died on 5 June 1955. John was well cared for and wanted for nothing enjoying all the comforts of a middle class upbringing. He suffered another huge blow on 15 July 1958 when his mother was knocked down and killed by a speeding motorist as she crossed Menlove Avenue just minutes after visiting Mimi. John was at Blomfield Road at the time where he had been visiting his sisters. Julia was just forty four when she died. John attended Mosspits Lane Primary School for six months before being transferred to Dovedale Road Primary School,and on passing the eleven plus examination enrolled at Quarry Bank High School in September 1952. An undistinguished spell at Quarry Bank, which saw him fail all his O'Levels was followed by him being accepted by the Liverpool College of Art in Hope Street in September 1957. It was here that he would meet his future wife Cynthia and form close friendships with Stuart Sutcliffe, Bill Harry and Rod Murray who would meet regularly in Ye Cracke pub in nearby Rice Street. John moved in for a while with Stuart, Rod Murray and another student Rod Jones at a flat at Hillary Mansions, 3 Gambier Terrace directly opposite the Anglican Cathedral. Contrary to popular belief that he never had a so called proper job his sister Julia says John did work for a short while at the New Bears Paw Bar in Dorans Lane off Lord Street where his stepfather Bobby Dykins was restaurant manager. John and Cynthia married at the registry office at 64 Mount Pleasant and lived for a while in Brian Epstein's flat at 36 Falkner Street. The wedding reception took place at Reeces Restaurant.

John Lennon was murdered by Mark Chapman in New York on 8 December 1980.

9 Newcastle Road where John
spent an ealy part of his childhiooid
near Penny Lane (above)

Working Class hero? John's favourite
home Mendips - he shared with Aunt
Mimi and later Cynthia. (above)

John Lennon was a home bird.
He certainly enjoyed his growing up in
Newcastle Road around the corner from
Penny Lane and later when he lived with
his Aunt Mimi in the house called
Mendips.
Visitors to the home – now owned by the
National Trust- on the daily Beatle tours
are always surprised by the plush,leafy
South Liverpool area where it is situated.
To many it doesn't reflect John's 'working
class hero' tag when they see it.
Mendips was ideal for John he could stroll
to Quarry Bank school.
He would also play truant at the nearby
Strawberry Field orphanage.
John was fiercely proud of his Scouse
roots as backed up by Yoko Ono when she
officially opened John Lennon Airport.
She visited his childhood haunts when she
first came to Liverpool along with Sean.
John also made a point of singing about
Lime Street in the Beatle version of
Maggie Mae.
It is said that at the bottom of his bed at
the Dakota Building in New York he had a
sea chest that had stamped on it one word
'LIVERPOOL'.
He also kept his school tie and wore it at
parties.
Many close to him said it was his dream to
return to Liverpool sailing into the
Mersey and the waterfront and coming
home on a visit.
He remained a dreamer.
But John's song In My Life sums up just
what the streets of Liverpool meant to
him.

A happy productive post Sgt
Pepper period for John (above)

NEWCASTLE ROAD

9 NEWCASTLE ROAD

...nce Albt. tramdriv...
...nael Jn. Rd. foreman

NEWCASTLE ROAD, WAVERTREE (15
Church rd. to 7 Charles Berrington rd
LEFT SIDE.
1 Edwards Geo. Bruce
3 Hamilton Mrs. Gladys France
5 Whittingham Jn. Wm
7 East Mrs. Alice Steele
9 Stanley Mrs. Mary
11 Hesketh Hy
11A Pye Wm. foreman bricklyr
15 Chapman Jack storekeeper
17 Jackson Wltr. railwayman
21 Mensing George seaman
23 Rushworth Wm. engnr
25 Stewart Wm. civil engnr

ARTHUR ASKEY

The one time choir boy, civil servant and a multi-talented Liverpudlian whom Ken Dodd called a 'giant of a man'. He was 'Little but big-hearted' Arthur Askey.

SANDHURST STREET

SANDHURST ST. Toxteth Park
48 Bassandona Harry assist.scho
50 Roe Arthur traveller
52 Johnston Thomas cashier
54 Derney Thomas mariner
56 Robinson Mrs. Jane
58 **Askey Samuel book keeper**
60 Foggo Thomas manager
62 Thomas John A.
64 Christian Jn. Wm. marine en
66 Taggart Richard
68 Hannah Robert joiner
70 Roddan Samuel
72 Evans Robert builder
74 Boulton Robert foreman
76 Thompson Robert R. yard fo
78 Dean John zinc worker

One of the greatest Liverpool comedians was born at 19 Moses Street, Dingle on the 6 June 1900 – Arthur Bowden Askey.

This area is often referred to as the 'Holy Land' due to the name of the surrounding streets – Moses, Isaac, Jacob and David.

They are all still standing today.

Arthur's father, Samuel was a general merchant's bookkeeper who was married to Betsy. They also had a younger daughter, Irene. The Askeys moved to 90 Rosslyn Street, Aigburth and then the short distance to 58 Sandhurst Street. Arthur was educated firstly at St Michael's in-the-Hamlet Primary School from which he gained a scholarship to the Liverpool Institute High School in Mount Street.

The 'Inny' has boasted many celebrities amongst its ex pupils including in later years, George Harrison, Paul McCartney and Bill Kenwright.

It is said that Arthur and Paul sat at the same desk although 40 years apart, and that Paul sent him a telegram many years later which said 'From the guy who inherited your old desk.It is still there with your name carved on it'!

Arthur left at 16 and started working at the Liverpool Education Offices at 14 Sir Thomas Street. He was responsible for handing out official documents to the parents of children due to have operations.

He jokingly referred to this as the tonsils and adenoids department.

Around this time he met his future wife May Swash who worked at Goodlass Wall and Co, The Strand near the Pier Head.

Every morning they travelled to work together by train from Aigburth to Liverpool Central Station.

They married on 23 March 1939 at St Michael-in the Hamlet Church, Aigburth where Arthur had been a chorister as a child and they had one daughter, Anthea who became an actress.

By now Arthur had entered the world of show business and he went on to become one of the country's best loved comics.

He was universally known as big-hearted Arthur and for his catchphrase 'Hello Playmates'.

May died in 1974 and Arthur went to live with his sister Irene in Kensington, London.

From all accounts May was an extremely shy person and never really adapted to being connected to show business life.

Arthur's own health deteriorated and in June 1982. Sadly, the strain of two major leg operations so close to each other proved too much at his age,and he passed away in a London Hospital on 16 November 1982. He was 82 years of age.

He once said: "There's a sign on the wall where I was born – on it it says 'Condemned'."

"I thang you..." Waxing lyrical Arthur and his model at Madame Tussauds (opposite)and life in the 'Holy Land '(above).

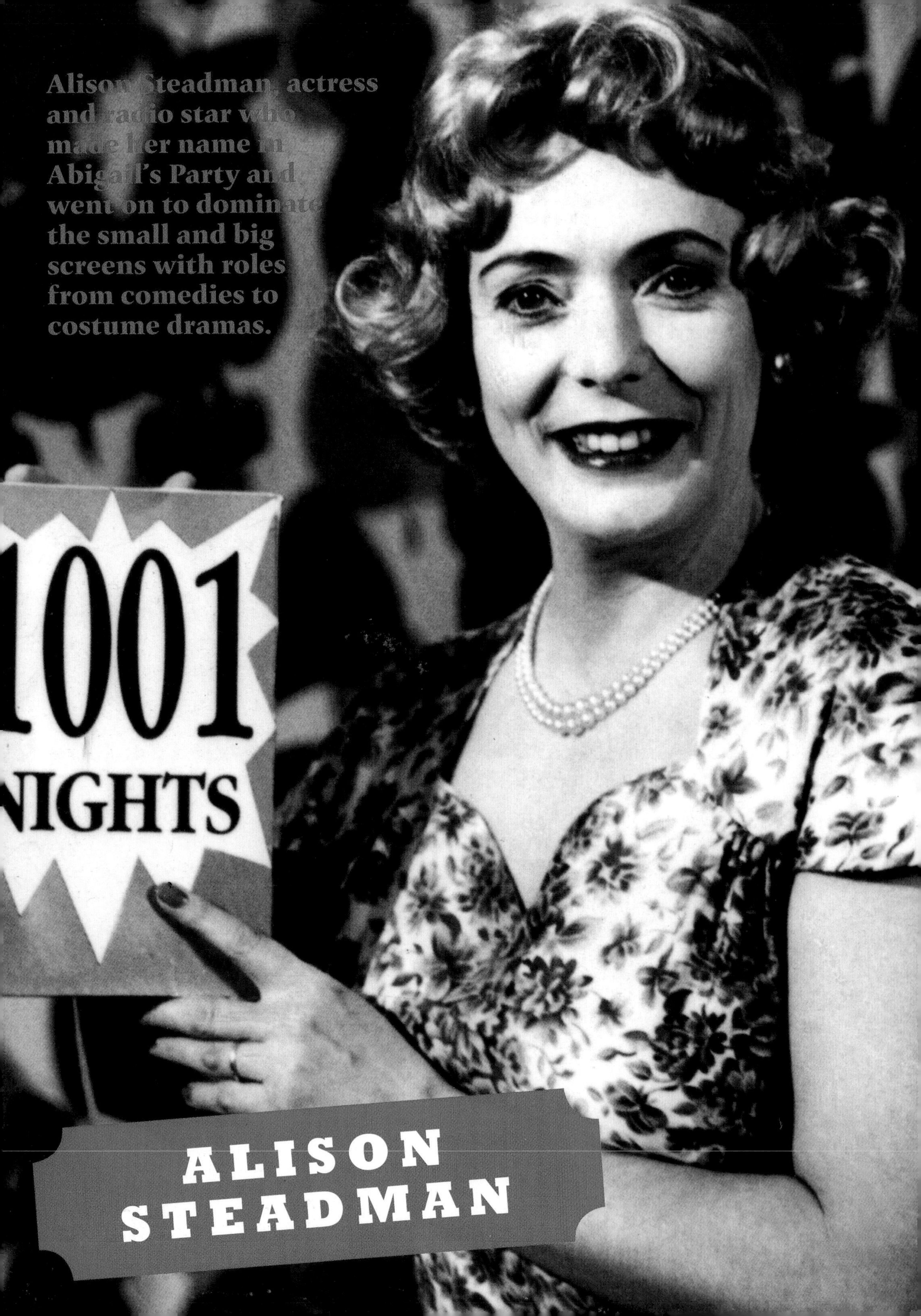

Alison Steadman, actress and radio star who made her name in Abigail's Party and went on to dominate the small and big screens with roles from comedies to costume dramas.

1001 NIGHTS

ALISON STEADMAN

The daughter of George Percival Steadman and Margaret, Alison was born on 26 August 1946 the youngest of three girls.

The family home was at 4 Sherwyn Road in Anfield. She attended Childwall Valley High School for Girls in Childwall Valley Road and on leaving school at sixteen, worked for a while for the Liverpool Probation Service at 3a Crosshall Street as a secretary.

During her lunch break she would visit the Cavern Club to see her favourite band The Beatles.

One day she and a friend followed John Lennon and Paul McCartney and caught up with them at the main Post Office in Victoria Street.

She obtained Paul's autograph who spelt her name Alison incorrectly with two ls and signed it 'Paul.'

Having second thoughts, he crossed out Paul and replaced it with 'Beatles' saying "It looked better as no one would know who Paul was in the years to come!"

From a young age she had nurtured ambitions to be an actress and loved doing impressions of people.

When she went to her drama school audition she sneaked off from work but her colleagues in the Probation office were very supportive and her boss remarked that what ever she did with the rest of her life she had to get away from there.She trained to become an actress at the East Acton School in London.

Since then she has gone on to become an accomplished actress in stage, TV and films winning numerous awards including the prestigious Evening Standard Best Actress Award in 1977. She has also won a BAFTA on two occasions. Her many roles have included Beverly in 'Abigail's Party' and as Mrs Bennet in the BBC series Pride and Prejudice. She has also appeared as a comedy actress on radio in such programmes as Eddy Braben's 'The Show With Eight Legs' and 'News Huddlines'.

She now lives in Highgate,London and has two sons Toby born in 1979 and Leo in 1981.

She married Mike Leigh in 1973 and the couple divorced in 2001.

On July 15 each year she visits Liverpool to have lunch with her sisters Sylvia and Pamela – and to visit the graves of their parents.

Three faces of Alison Steadman.
The versatile actress can tackle any role as shown by these three divers images from her career

SHERWYN ROAD

..D, ANFIELD (4).
..d to Hildebrand road.
RIGHT SIDE.
..s Geo. Wm. mechanic
..rwick Albt. clerk
..mpbell Mrs. Lilian
..artledge Jn. Thos. foreman
..Byrne Fredk. clerk
..2 Bartlett Jsph. Hy. clerk
14 Mason Harold Dean civil servant
16 Beesley Wm. engnr
18 Arnot Wm. Edwd. motor driver
20 Forrest Thos. tea salesman
22 Steadman Geo. P. clerk
24 Gray Arth. Sinclair
26 Griffith Alfd
28 Thompson Geo. plumber
30 Morley Edwd. Ernest electrician
32 Rothwell Laurence saw mkr.
34 Roberts Elwy Clwyd travllr

JEAN ALEXANDER

Jean Alexander is one of the nation's favourite actresses from the soap Coronation Street to sitcom Last of The Summer Wine – she is a lovely lady and a natural, modest star.

The family lived in Rhiwlas Street, one of the so called Welsh streets off High Park Street in the Toxteth area of Liverpool.

Born Jean Hodgkinson in October 1926 the year of the general strike, she was the youngest of two children, her elder brother Ken was born in 1924.

Her father Archibald Alexander Hodgkinson was a ship electrical engineer who worked on ships all over the country and was often away from home for up to three months at a time.

They would later reside in Harrowby Street and then at 37 Arnold Street.

Due to her mother's encouragement Jean was able to read before she started school.

Her first school was Upper Park Street Primary off Park Road then Granby Street Junior School where she was in the same class as Lita Roza.

On passing the scholarship she attended St Edmund's, Princes Park where she enjoyed playing hockey, tennis and netball.

An avid reader it was perhaps appropriate that on leaving school she worked for the Library service for five years firstly in Windsor Street, Toxteth and Everton Library.

In her spare time she enjoyed visiting the Rialto Theatre in Berkley Street with her brother Ken. In 1949 she commenced working in the theatre on a full time basis and left Liverpool to live and work in London.

Jean had by now adopted the surname Alexander which was her father's middle name.

She has lived in Southport since 1970 in a semi detached house where she enjoys tending the garden and shopping on Lord Street.

Jean is perhaps best known as Hilda Ogden in Coronation Street a part she played for 23 years.

In Coronation Street she was famous for her headscarf and Jean as a young girl remembers women travelling to the munition factory in Speke wearing similar headgear.

Like her character Hilda most of them would also have curlers in their hair. However, unlike Hilda, Jean has never married.

Since 1988 she has been a mainstay as Auntie Wainwright in the long running comedy series 'Last of The Summer Wine'. Despite now being in her eighties she is still full of energy and continues to be much in demand. When time permits she indulges herself by taking holidays on cruise ships.

Jean Alexander Liverpool actress and one time librarian (opposite);
Jean in her youth (top above);
The much-loved Hilda Ogden (above).

RHIWLAS STREET

...ssist. storekeeper
...ll Steele draughtsman
...dward plumber
RIGHT SIDE.
...he Alexander Martin
...askell Frederick shop assistant
Williams Edwin clerk
Williams Mrs. Mary
8 Wilson Thomas gas collector
10 Gililand Reginald clerk
12 Hayes Thomas bricksetter
14 Owen Richard mariner
16 Robson James shipwright
18 Hodgkinson Archibald electrician
20 McLean James baker
22 Freeman Arthur John manager
24 Rogers George engineer
26 Marley John warehouseman
28 Kindlen Mrs. Ellen
30 Williams Mrs. Catherine
32 Cumpsty Mrs. Agnes Lydia
34 Williams Mrs. Margaret
... Robinson James Lemon warehousman

EDDIE
BRABEN

A former market worker, this naturally funny man lived for making people laugh at work. Eddie Braben was later a much sought after writer working for Doddy and Morecambe and Wise.

Eddie was born in Monkswell Street, Liverpool 8 in 1930 and attended Mathew Arnold School in Dingle Lane.

Arguably Britain's best comedy writer, Eddie an unsung genius wrote jokes for Ken Dodd for twelve years and then Morecambe and Wise for fourteen.

The latter were Britain's most famous but demanding double act in Britain and Eddy had to work to a strict time table.

They have placed on record their appreciation of his influence on their careers in show business.

In 1940 he was evacuated to the village of Gaurwen on Anglesey,staying there for the duration of the Second World War.

As a child he was entranced by comedians on the radio particularly Arthur Askey. On his return to Liverpool he commenced working at Ogden's Tobacco Factory in West Derby Road.

It was here that the young Eddie would listen to the ad libbing of his workmates, much of which he would remember in later years when writing scripts for the various stars.

A born observer, Eddie describes his time at Ogden's as being educated at the 'The University Of Life '. His father was a butcher in St John's Market and Eddie would also help out on the stall, coming into contact with Liverpool characters which also influenced his future material.

It was whilst working at the market that he began writing jokes taking a note pad to work each day and writing down anything he thought was amusing. He would send his material to comedians who were appearing in Liverpool, his first success was selling some to Charlie Chester for 2s 6d.

He served his National Service at RAF Kenley, Surrey in the cookhouse which was yet another productive grounding for his future career.

Another great influence was his distant relative the legendary 'Vaudeville' artist Billy Matchett also from Liverpool and Eddie was a frequent visitor to his home in Booker Avenue, Mossley Hill. Eddie was also influential in Carla Lane's early career.

He was then living at 45 Honeygreens Lane in West Derby and Carla lived close by in Eaton Road. She appreciated his words of encouragement and helpful advice. Eddie moved with his wife Dee to the Snowdonia National Park in the 1970's but remains in close contact with Liverpool through his tireless work for charities in the city which include The Salvation Army and Alder Hey Children's Hospital. He has won numerous awards for his writing.

Eddie Braben checks another kind of material (opposite); Bringing us sunshine (above) writer for Eric and Ernie.

FLW 44

JOHN
GORMAN

A member of Scaffold and the show Tiswas and his own theatre company. John Gorman came a long way from the funny man who sold fish over the phone and then flogged encyclopaedias door-to-door. He now encourages poetry.

One of three children John was born on 4 January 1936 in Cleveland Street, Birkenhead to John and Elizabeth Gorman.

When he was two the family moved to 34 Beckwith Street. He attended St Laurence's in Park Street and then St Anselm's College, Manor Hill, Claughton.

On leaving school he worked for the GPO firstly in Palm Grove, Birkenhead and then at Lancaster House in Castle Street, Liverpool as a technical officer where at the age of 22 he was put in charge of a department. He had also served his National Service in the RAF. He moved to a basement flat in Princess Avenue, Liverpool 8 before leaving the city to work in Dublin for a brief period. Returning to Liverpool he had a variety of jobs which included Associated Fisheries and Foods in Walton selling fish to customers over the phone and then selling the Encyclopedia Brittanica door-to-door.

A further period of employment at the GPO this time in Huyton followed.Throughout this period he had been involved in amateur dramatics and in 1960 he attended the Playhouse theatre for an audition responding to an advert for non equity parts. He was given a small part in the play Luther the 16th century reforming monk which in view of his strict Catholic education he now finds somewhat ironic! Thus began his long association with the Merseyside arts scene.

A chance meeting with Adrian Henri, Arthur Dooley and Arthur Ballard at the Jacaranda in Slater Street saw him involved in the 1962 Merseyside Arts Festival which led to him performing sketches with Roger McGough and Mike McCartney at the Blue Angel Club in Seel Street, which was run by Allan Williams.

The trio soon became known as The Scaffold a name stumbled upon by Roger McGough when looking through Roget's Thesaurus.

The Scaffold went on to achieve huge chart success including a UK number one hit Lily The Pink" in 1968 and in all released thirteen singles and eight albums. The group disbanded in 1974 with each member pursuing individual careers but they have remained good friends to this day. Between 1978 and 1981 John appeared in the popular children's TV show TISWAS in 80 editions.

Since then he has worked as a director for entertainment programmes on London Weekend Television and after a period living in France he returned as artistic director tor The Theatre On The Steps in Bridgnorth,Shropshire. He returned to Birkenhead in 2005 and is still actively involved in the local arts scene.

A fair cop – madcap capers with fellow Scaffolders (opposite);
On stage with Mike McGear and Roger McGough (above)

ROBB WILTON

One of the great Liverpool comedians. An inspiration to many. His sharp delivery and ability to communicate to all ages lives on.

Robb was christened Robert Smith and was born 28 August 1881 at 81 Warburton Street, Brownlow Hill. His father Joseph was a compositor with the Manchester Guardian and the old Liverpool Courier. Robbs stage talent was probably inherited from his mother Elizabeth who had been an actress. As a lad he was an altar boy at St Mary's Church in Walton. On leaving school he had a variety of jobs including at Victory Engineering works in Tunnel Road and at Turners Nurseries in Garston. It was in Garston that he made his first stage appearance at The Theatre Royal but it was at a theatre of the same name in Anfield that he discovered his talent for comedy. The theatre was known as The 'Blood Tub' as it staged several violent melodramas each week. Robb spent over three years there and then took engagements at the Lyric in Everton and the Pavilion in New

Brighton. It was at the Pavilion that he was spotted by the impresario Sir Walter de Frece who had been educated at the Liverpool Institute ,and Robb's professional career then took off at a great pace. Paul McCartney recalls obtaining his autograph and John Lennon was a huge fan attending his shows at the Empire after a day at Art College. By now he was married to Florence Palmer and their first home was at 3 Redcar Street, Clubmoor. The couple were inseparable and in the early years would appear together on stage. Robb was inconsolable when Florence died in February 1956. He became a household name during the Second World War because of his radio broadcasts which usually began with the words 'The day the war broke out, my missus said to me '. He continued to be much in demand in the post war years but as his wifes health deteriorated he cut down on his engagements, and the couple went to live with Reginald Breach and his wife at 30 Mayville Road in Aigburth. Robb became president of the Liverpool Archery Club and Vice-President of the Liverpool Supporters Club. He died in Broadgreen Hospital, his funeral taking place at St Margaret's Church in Rocky Lane, Anfield on 6 May 1957. In June 1959 a plaque to his memory was placed on the wall of the foyer at the Liverpool Royal Court.

Ken Dodd has described Robb as one of the greatest influences on his career.

A comedy genius - Robb Wilton and the
art of communicating (opposite);
Young Robb (above)

BROOKSIDE CLOSE

Close encounters of the Brookie kind. For 20 years this 'star street', created by Phil Redmond, brought Liverpool more fame

Adrian was born on 10 April 1932 at Sidney Buildings, Sidney Street, Higher Tranmere and later lived at Mount Street Liverpool 1.

His grandfather was a seaman from Mauritius who had settled in Birkenhead and ran the Seaman's Mission.

He was also an accomplished dancer and worked as a dancing instructor.

The young Adrian could see the Liverpool skyline from his bedroom window and spent many hours watching the city being attacked during World War Two.

He was fascinated with the bright colours in the sky and would later say that this influenced his life long love of painting.

In 1941 he was evacuated to Rhyl in North Wales and attended St Asaph Grammar School where he found himself the only pupil studying A Level Art, and consequently had the classroom to himself.

For a short while he worked on a market stall in Rhyl and also at the fairground.

After studying art at Kings College, Newcastle he lectured in the subject at various establishments including the Liverpool College of Art in Hope Street. In 1972 he won first prize in the prestigious John Moores Art Competition.

In 1967 he formed the 'Liverpool Scene' who released 4 LP's the first one being produced by John Peel. One of three poets with Roger McGough and Brian Patten he was also a member of the Merseysound.

In the late 1990s Adrian had a major stroke which severely limited his ability to communicate but he fought back and with the help and encouragement of his partner of 15 years Cathy Marcangeli.

He was writing and painting again.

They lived at 21 Mount Street, directly opposite LIPA in Hope Street.

However he suffered a heart attack and died on 21 December 2000.

A larger-than-life character, he said that there was nowhere he loved better or felt at home than Liverpool. The city recognised his cultural contribution by bestowing on him several honours including the Freedom of the City in company with fellow scribes Roger McGough and Brian Patten, shortly before his death. Perhaps fittingly the last poem he wrote was entitled 'Coronary Care Unit'. Adrian had lived in the Liverpool 8 area since 1957 and had resided at a number of addresses including 64 Canning Street and latterly at 21 Mount Street. He would spend a lot of time in Ye Cracke pub in Rice Street and also later at O'Connor's in Mount Pleasant. I think he would have been honoured and amused to have a pub listed as his residence rather than an actual address! O'Connor's was Adrian's spiritual home in the late sixties and seventies and its dour interior was a meeting place for some of the most creative talent in the city. Sadly, no more but Adrian's legacy lives on.

Adrian in his studio (opposite);
Recovering from an illness
(above left);
the cover of the Mersey Sound
(above right).

Adrian Henri,
poet, painter, performer
enjoyed passing on his
skills to schools and
universities.
He loved attending
the opening of any
new exhibition
especially those
heralding
Merseyside's
creative talent.

ADRIAN HENRI

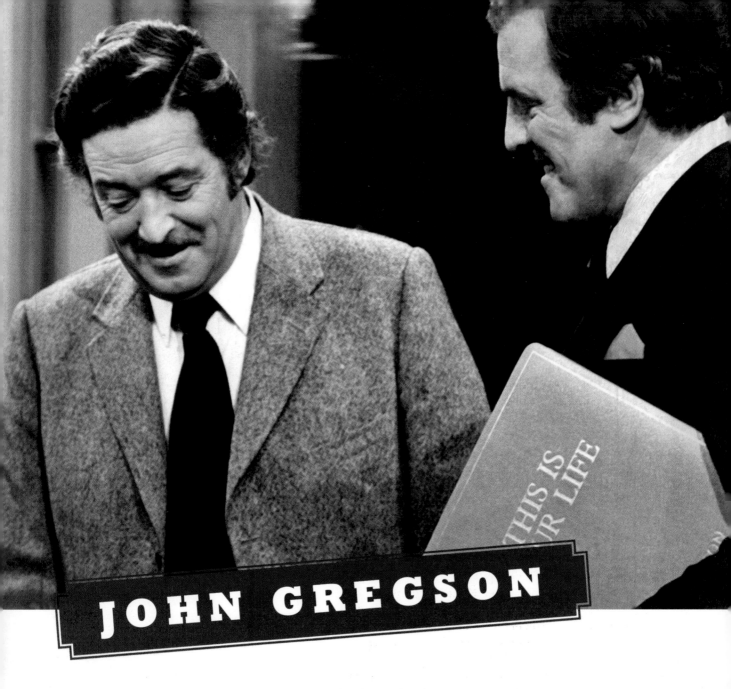

JOHN GREGSON

One of the most respected actors to emerge from Liverpool. He was a star of stage, TV and big screen. He could put his hand to any role and John Lennon was a big fan.

The Gregson family lived at 1 Crawford Avenue in Wavertree L15 and John attended St Francis Xavier School, Salisbury Street in the city centre. Born 15 March 1919 the youngest of three boys and two girls he was christened Harold Thomas Gregson.

He left school at the age of 14 when he started work at the Automatic Telephone Manufacturing Company in Edge Lane before moving on to work as a draughtsman for Liverpool Corporation in the Cleansing Department. His father Ernest, a road surveyor with the Liverpool Corporation, died suddenly when John was sixteen and because of the need of a steady income the family moved to a larger house and took in students as lodgers. Called up for the Second World War he served on minesweepers sustaining a serious injury but he continued in his duties until the end of the hostilities.

On his return to civilian life he joined the Liverpool Old Vic Company based at the Liverpool Playhouse Theatre and was given several bit parts. He then spent a period on the dole in Liverpool before his acting career really took off in 1958 when he played a petty officer in the highly successful film ' Scott Of The Antartic '.

John Gregson surprised by Eamonn Andrews on This is Your Life (opposite);
A publicity shot for the great actor (above).

His career inevitably took him away from Liverpool but he was a regular visitor to the city to visit his brother Ernest who lived at 36 Alexandra Drive in Aigburth, and his sisters Stella from Morningside, Crosby and Chris in Limedale Road, Mossley Hill.

He also had a Beatles connection for in the late 1950s a then virtually unknown John Lennon who was in Ye Cracke Pub in Rice Street spotted the actor pull up in his car and asked for his autograph. Looking around for something for him to sign he allegedly spotted an old boot and much to John Lennon's amusement he signed it across the stitching allegedly writing ' I get a kick out of you '. He was regular visitor to the Cavern Club when it first opened indulging in his life long interest in jazz music. His nephew Arthur Johnson worked at the Liverpool Echo for many years and now has his own PR company.

John Gregson suffered a heart attack on 8 January 1975 at his Somerset home and died leaving behind his wife and six children. He was just 55 years of age.

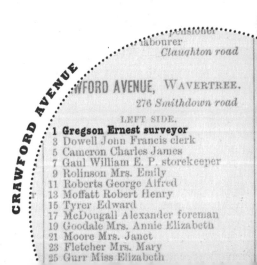

CLIVE HORNBY

A 60s pop star became an Emmerdale soap hero. Clive Hornby had a huge following in no matter what he did. TV's Mr Nice Guy.

Clive was born on 20 October 1944 in the Walton district of Liverpool. The family home was in Bull Lane off Orrell Lane.

He attended Warbreck Secondary School in Longmoor Lane which was rumoured to have been built by Mr Hartley the 'jam man' for his workers children in 1896. It had laid derelict for a number of years after being amalgamated with Evered High School otherwise known as Fazakerly High.

The school later became Longmoor Lane Junior due to a fire at nearby Rice Lane Primary when the children were transferred to the building in Longmoor Lane. The building was demolished in 2000 and a new school now stands next door.

On leaving school Clive trained as an accountant for six months but hating the nine to five regime he joined the Liverpool Playhouse working behind the scenes. With his friends Ray Scragg, Eddy Parry, Steve McClaren and Alan Willis he formed the 60s Merseybeat band The Dennisons who took their name from Dennison Street off Great Howard Street. Clive was the drummer.

They were dubbed the baby Beatles as they were three or four years younger than the originals and had similar hair styles.

They played on the same bill as The Beatles on five occasions and also had a Saturday night residency at the BICC social club in Melling. They disbanded in 1967 but not before achieving two minor hits with 'Walkin The Dog' and ' Come On Be My Girl' both on the Decca label. A third single released in November 1964 'Nobody Like My Babe' failed to chart.

Clive then trained to become an actor and has played Jack Sugden in the long running TV soap Emmerdale since 1979. The series had started life as Emmerdale Farm changing its name to just Emmerdale in 1993.

Malandra Borrows (stage name Burrows) also from Liverpool was also a regular in the soap for a number of years. She was born Malandra Newman and is from the Woolton area of the city. Clive married Helen Weir who played his wife Pat in the series ,and the couple lived in Yorkshire.

A keen supporter of Liverpool FC he said he owed the city a lot especially the council who gave him a mature students' grant enabling him to become a drama student.

Clive died in 2008.

Clive Hornby on a TV set (opposite)

McGANNS

Sometimes called 'The Other Fab Four' Liverpool's very versatile stars The McGann men have taken stage, TV and film by storm while sister Clare works behind the scenes.

You would be hard pressed to find so much talent in one family. All five of Joseph and Clare McGanns family have been successful in TV and the acting profession. Their eldest son Joe was born in 1958, Paul in 1959, Mark 1961, Stephen 1963 and Clare in 1965 Two other children Joseph and John died at birth. Raised in Birstall Road in the Kensington area of Liverpool, their father Joseph was a metallurgist who had served in the Second World War with the Royal Naval Commandos and after the war also worked in various local factories. Their mother was a teacher who was a lover of literature and read Shakespeare to her children when they were young. This and their fathers advice to avoid factory work and shift work at all costs no

Fredk   *Winford st*

BIRSTALL ROAD

STALL ROAD, KENSINGTON
17 *Thornes road.*

LEFT SIDE.

1ᴀWholesale Pet Products who.
  foods
1 McCann Mrs. A
2 Heffey Mrs. Catherine
3 Baldwin Mrs. Emma
4 **McGann Jsph**   Mᶜ GANNS
5 Gardner Jas
6 McDowall Albt
7 Roberts Mrs. M
8 Williams Mrs. Winifred
9 Linton Mrs. Eliz
10 Ravenscroft Henshall
11 Wilson Thos
12 Woods Thos. J
13 Abrahams H. tailor
   Lynch Herbt

doubt influenced their choice of future careers. They were brought up quite strictly in the Catholic faith and Paul attended Cardinal Heenan Catholic Grammar School. The family were also very musical and the boys sang in choirs as children. They would later form a group and record several records. All the brothers appeared in the TV programme 'The Hanging Gale' an account of the Irish Potato Famine. Paul has had the most notable acting career, studying at RADA, after working for the DSS in Liverpool and became the eighth Dr Who in 1996 for a joint US/UK production about the time lord although it never became a series. His performance as Percy Topliss in Alan Bleasdales 'The Monocled Mutineer' put him in line for a major TV award. Mark gave an excellent portrayal of John Lennon at the Everyman theatre and has been involved in many musicals. He hosted the John Lennon songbook concert at the Philharmonic Hall in July 2008. Stephen as well as being an actor is a writer and has written scripts for the popular TV series 'The Bill'. He also featured in the BBC TV sitcom ' Help'. Joe has appeared in several TV series including 'Casualty' and 'Heartbeat'. Joe the eldest child is a talented singer and songwriter. The only daughter Clare is a TV producer. They all remain proud of their Liverpool roots despite living in other parts of the country, and are keen fundraisers for various charities including the NSPCC for whom Stephen and Joe undertook a sponsored walk across Peru in 1999.

The McGanns on stage in Yakety Yak (opposite); Stephen (top left) On cue, Paul (above left); Joe (centre); and Mark (right).

RICHARD CODMAN

Punch and Judy is known the world over. The roots of this timeless company are from the streets of Liverpool.

EGYPT STREET

surance agent
warehouseman
Geo. Fredk. timber sales
The Sh

EGYPT ST.—E
2 Arrad
LEFT SIDE.
Noble James & Sons painters
1 Eagle Michael milk carter
Nile place
17 Cohen Gerald marine store dealer
Mulberry st
RIGHT SIDE.
10 **Codman Rd. Punch & Judy** entert

ELAINE ST.—S
143 Windsor
LEFT SIDE.
Whittick Randle Harry draper
Craigie Miss Jane R., L.L.

The Codman family of Romany origin arrived in Liverpool in the 1860s and their first Punch and Judy site in 1868 was originally in St George's Square near Lime Street on a roundabout called the Quadrant – an open cobbled square which was between The North Western Hotel and the main railway station (now known as Lime Street) and St John's Market. The site was described as the only one of its kind in the United Kingdom. Richard Codman was a circus traveller from Norwich who was born in 1832 and died in 1909. He had three sons, two of whom carried on the tradition, Richard junior took over the Quadrant site and Herbert, who was younger, took responsibility for the Llandudno site on the North Welsh coast which had been founded a few years earlier. Richard the third was equally successful as his grandfather and father and in 1922 the Sandon's Studio Society an artistic body in Liverpool commissioned the famous Liverpool sculptor Tyson-Smith to wood carve a magnificent Punch and Judy booth. After Richard's death in 1951, Richard the fourth continued in his forebears traditions until his death in 1985 when Ronald born in Liverpool in 1928 the sixth generation of the Codman dynasty took over from his father. Unfortunately the famous Lime Street site no longer exists due to redevelopment. The show was temporarily housed inside St George's Hall and occasionally Williamson Square near the Playhouse Theatre. It was based at Liverpool Museum of Life at the Albert Dock along with one of Richard Codman's 19th century original puppet booths. Also exhibited were some of the original characters. The Codman family lived at 10 Egypt Street near Hardman Street and later at 44 Farnworth Street, Liverpool 6.

That's the way to do it... the Codman generation in action (opposite); Now this is not a puppet, a Codman and a cute canine (right).

The Mersey Cowboy. Charlie Landsborough –
the storyteller from the banks of Birkenhead
to Nashville.

CHARLIE LANDSBOROUGH

Charlie Landsborough – singer-songwriter. The Birkenhead cowboy was a very late star starter. In 1995 when he was into his fifties he made his big break and became a leading light in the world's country and western scene.

Born Charles Alexander Landsborough on 26 October 1941 in Wrexham, where the family had briefly gone to escape the heavy bombing that was inflicted on Birkenhead during that year.

They returned shortly afterwards to their home at 25 Observatory Road in the dock area of the town.

Charlie is the youngest of eleven children all of whom were musical, a talent they inherited from their parents .He attended local schools and his poor educational record was blamed on his obsession with the banjo which he had learned to play at an early age.

His mother Aggie died when Charlie was just twelve years of age and he left school early.

He had a variety of jobs including working on the railways and at a local flour mill.

He was also an apprentice telephone engineer for a short while.

He then enlisted as a regular soldier and it was while he was serving in Germany that he began playing in bands. Fed up with Army life, after four years he bought himself out and worked for a brief while as a postman in Coventry.

He returned to Germany and joined The Chicago Sect Band and it was during this period that he married Thelma his childhood sweetheart whom he had known since his schooldays.

On his return to Birkenhead he had a number of jobs before commencing teaching in 1980 at Laird Street Primary School.

In the evenings he was performing at Birkenhead pubs including the North Western in Cleveland Street, and the Pacific in Price Street were he sang for over 20 years.

A very late starter it was not until 1995 and then into his fifties that he made his big break into the country and western scene but he has since toured all over the world as well as making many TV appearances.

He recorded an album in Nashville in 1999 and is extremely popular in the United States where he spends much of his time.

Most of his albums have topped the British Country charts.

And he also has a large following in Ireland.

On a recent visit to Birkenhead and learning that the family home in Observatory Road was boarded up and due for demolition, he climbed in and was amazed at how small it actually was and how such a large family had managed to live in such cramped conditions.

OBSERVATORY ROAD

.ss. W
Jas
.ust Ernest
.Nulty Patrick Jsph
9 Titley Fredk
11 Colley Wm
13 Smith Alfd. O
15 Alldis Mrs. E
17 Jones Wltr
19 McComb Hy
21 Rogers Fredk
23 Cook Mrs. E
25 Landsborough Jas
27 Miller Wm. G
29 Molloy Mrs. Mary
31 Brooks Jas
33 Cunningham Patrick J
35 Wright Mrs. R
37 Kelly Stephen
39 McKee Geo
41 Davis Alfd. E

BREAD

JEAN BOHT

'Bread winner,' Jean Boht played Ma Boswell in the long-running saga of a real scouse family. A real Liverpool Institution and a critically-acclaimed straight actress.

Jean Dance was born in Liverpool on 6 March 1936. She was brought up in Acreville Road, Bebington where she attended local schools leaving at the age of seventeen. The family later moved to 35 Beresford Avenue in Lower Bebington. Her father was a manufacturer's agent for a confectionery firm and also ran an amateur dramatic group in which Jean and her younger sister, Maureen, would act. Jean became a professional actress at the Liverpool Playhouse in 1961.

She has happy memories of spending a large slice of her weekly wage of £1 on posh teas at the Adelphi Hotel. Her mother Teddy Dance who died in 1990 aged 82 was a celebrity in her own right, playing the piano outside Marks and Spencers in Basnett Street for a number of years raising money for cancer charities which included £56,000 for a scanner at Clatterbridge Hospital.

A plaque to her memory was laid on a paving stone outside the store.

Jean's father had died from cancer at a relatively young age.

Jean of course made her mark as the mother of one of the most famous TV families of all time – the Boswells in Carla Lane's Bread which was set in the Dingle.

Her success as Nellie Boswell owes some of its inspiration to a woman she met whilst travelling on the train from Lime Street to Runcorn.

The woman worked in a bra factory and entertained Jean with hilarious stories about the factory and which bras went to which shops.

Jean also has memories of going round Liverpool when her father was visiting clients and being fascinated by people, who despite living in poor conditions had so much energy living their lives to the utmost, and fiercely protective of their families.

She is married to Carl Davies the American composer and conductor of the Liverpool Philharmonic's summer pops. The couple have two daughters Hannah and Jessie Jo. Although she now lives in the South of England she is a regular visitor to Merseyside and supports many regional charities.

Ma Boswell aka Jean Boht in Carla Lane's comedy (opposite); Portrait of the actress as a young woman (above)

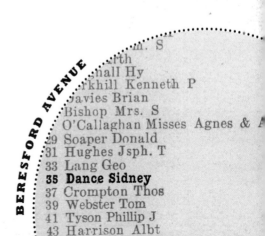

BERESFORD AVENUE
m. S
...rth
...nall Hy
...rkhill Kenneth P
...avies Brian
...Bishop Mrs. S
...O'Callaghan Misses Agnes & A
29 Soaper Donald
31 Hughes Jsph. T
33 Lang Geo
35 Dance Sidney
37 Crompton Thos
39 Webster Tom
41 Tyson Phillip J
43 Harrison Albt
45 Bailey Harold Geo

RICHARD STILGOE

He is a musician, writer, radio wit, presenter and the ideal guest for any chat show. So don't try and pigeon-hole the versatile Mr Stilgoe.

Richard was born in Camberly, Surrey on 28 March 1943 but was brought up in Liverpool his family having moved to the city in 1946. His father John was the Chief engineer for Liverpool Corporation and the family home was at 497 Aigburth Road and later at 5 St Anne's Road off Aigburth Road. He was educated at Liverpool College and once played on the same bill as the Beatles at the Cavern Club with his band "Tony Snow and the Blizzards". Richard was the lead singer and used the name Tony Snow. They appeared at several other venues on Merseyside including Litherland Town Hall where he recalls the band being pelted with bottle tops. They would play in red bow ties and white shirts and they were taken and collected from the gigs by their mothers ! As a boy he was a member of St Agnes' Church Choir in Ullet Road. A keen cricket fan he was a regular attender at Liverpool Cricket Club in Aigburth Road. On leaving school he won a Navy scholarship to Dartmouth but gave up after two weeks and

AIGBURTH ROAD

...ld E
...waite Thos. Arth
...ètt Eric Arth. C
...ilany G. J
...wyford Geo
O'Reilly Vincent, M.B., B.
  physcn. & surgn
Holmfield
471 Taylor Geo. Ivan chauffeur
473 Tinne P. Fredc., M.A., M.B., B.
  Oxon., M.R.C.S.Eng., L.R.(
  Lond. surgn
495 Jones Mrs. Mary Eli
497 Stilgoe Jn
499 Pollard Thos. Alfd. director
501 Browne Wm
503 Sanchez-Barona Enrique
  Aigburth Hall
  The Serpentine

THE BOULEVARD.
3 Webster Mrs. Charlotte A
  Oldham Sidney R S

went to Cambridge University instead, where at Clare College he obtained a degree in music. It was at Cambridge that he developed stage experience as a member of the University Foootlights Club. Fellow members included John Cleese, Graham Garden, Tim Brooke Taylor and Bill Oddie. Richard would later comment that if you cannot learn anything from that lot you may as well give up. As well as his musical talents he is an excellent wordsmith (he often points out to his audiences that his name is an anagram of Giscard O'Hitler). In the mid 1960s he linked up with Glyn Worsnip, and Bernard Falk who had been the rhythm guitarist with "Tony Snow and The Blizzards" and who had lived in Cooper Avenue North. Bernard Falk died in 1990. Richard's talents were perhaps best displayed in the popular BBC series 'Nationwide' and Esther Rantzen's 'That's Life'. He has lived in Surrey for a number of years and is a tireless charity worker most notably his founding of the Orpheus Centre which assists young disabled people in the performing arts. Still going strong Richard is a multi-talented performer be it as a playwright, poet, musician, lyricist or presenter.

Keyboard star Richard Stilgoe on stage (opposite);
Our learned friend at Liverpool JMU with his honorary degree (above).

PAUL McCARTNEY

The 'Scruff from Speke' is how Paul McCartney describes himself. A Beatle truely at home in Liverpool.

Paul was born on 18 June 1942 at Walton Hospital, Rice Lane, Liverpool 9. His mother Mary, a midwife, had once worked as a sister at the hospital and had qualified for a private ward for the birth of Paul. For most of his working life his father Jim was employed as a salesman at A. Hannay and Co., who had offices at 14 Chapel Street in the city centre. Mary was born Mary Patricia Mohin on 29 September 1909 at 2 Third Avenue, Fazakerly and Jim at 8 Fishguard Road, Everton on 7 July 1902. They were married on 15 April 1941 at St Swithin's Catholic Church in Gilmoss. Paul's younger brother Michael was born on 7 January 1944 also at Walton Hospital. After their wartime wedding in Mary and Jim moved into furnished rented rooms at 10 Sunbury Road, Anfield which was to be Paul's first home. A quick succession of homes followed – 92 Broadway, Wallasey, Roach Avenue, Knowsley, Sir Thomas White Gardens, Everton and then in 1949 to 72 Western Avenue, Speke. A further move was made in 1952 to 12 Ardwick Road, Speke before they finally settled at 20 Forthlin Road, Speke in 1955. This would remain home until 1964 when Paul bought his father Rembrandt a five bedroomed detached house in Baskervyle Road, Heswall. His mother had died on 31 October 1956 and is buried in Yew Tree Cemetery, Section 3a, Grave 276. Jim died in March 1976.

Paul's first school was Stockton Wood Road, Primary in Speke. Due to overcrowding both Paul and Michael were transferred to Joseph Williams Primary School in Sunnyfield Road, Gateacre . On passing his eleven plus examination Paul enrolled at the Liverpool Institute High School on 9 september 1953 and remained here until 21 July 1960 having obtained 5 GCE O'Levels and 1 A Level. The school ledger makes interesting reading , for under reason for leaving it reads ' Gone to work in Hamburg' ! The school building now houses the Liverpool Institute for Performing Arts or LIPA for short. This was Paul's brainchild and was opened in May 1996 by the Queen.

Paul worked briefly at Lewis's Department Store in Ranelagh Street as

a second mate on one of the store's delivery vans. Following the Beatles' first trip to Hamburg in 1960 he also worked briefly at Massey and Coggins – an electrical engineering firm in Bridge Road, Edge Hill which consisted of him winding coils for which he was paid £7 per week. The rest as they say is history!

He returned to the city on 1 June 2008 as part of the Capital of Culture celebrations and played before a sell out crowd at Liverpool Football Club's Anfield Stadium. He told the crowd that he had been born just down the road in Rice Lane and had lived less than a quarter of a mile from the stadium in Sunbury Road.

A Scosuer was home . . .

A Beatle relaxing in the summer of love
(opopsite) .
Peep show... a fan looking into Paul's past
(above) the Wings Commander on stage

WESTERN AVENUE

..... storekeeper
...ey Hugh
...ningham Rt. W
...oodroofe Rd. S. jeweller
    Crawford Rt. labourer
.2 Sawyer Wm. fitter
64 Wyness Edmnd. G.sheet metal wrkr
66 Rhodes Geo. Fredk. tool mkr
68 Coppock Rt. fitter

                        Blackrod av

70 Jones Rt. Maurice ship's steward
72 McCartney Mrs. Mary P. midwife
74 Cooper Herbt. Aug. fitter
76 Scarr H. M
78 Neilands Jas. L. fitter
80 Beattie Mrs. Elsie
82 Jeffery Harold T. fitter
84 Burgess Thos
86 Cahill Jsph. fitter
88 Starkey Edwd
90 Curtis Jsph
92 Hunter Mrs. Eliz
... Rylands ...

From Wavertree school boy to music legend, Holly Johnson has also enjoyed a solo career. He is now an accomplished artist.

William John Johnson was born in February 1960 at 186 Rathbone Road, Liverpool 15.

His name on his passport is William Holly Johnson.

The third child of Eric and Pat Johnson he has two brothers John and James, and a sister Clare. His father was a ship's steward whose parents ran a sweet shop near Edge Lane and his mother worked at various times at Plesseys and Meccano in Edge Lane, and was also an Avon lady.

A tight-knit family, his grandmother lived in Gladstone Road, Liverpool 7 and the young Johnson children spent a lot of time there.

William attended St Mary's School in Rathbone Road, where he sang in the church choir, and then the Liverpool Collegiate in Shaw Street.

The Collegiate does not hold happy memories for him as he was constantly goaded by other pupils because of his sexuality.

He truanted a lot and spent a lot of time at the Silver Blades Ice Rink in Prescot Road and the Regent Cinema in Old Swan.

In his late teens he would head to the City Centre to visit gay pubs such as the Lisbon in Victoria Street and the Bears Paw in Paddington. In the 1980's and now heavily into the punk scene he was a regular at Eric's Club in Mathew Street, firstly as a punter and then as a member of the 'Big in Japan' band who eventually became ' Frankie Goes To Hollywood ' named after Frank Sinatra. By now William was calling himself Holly and living at 46 Catherine Street, Liverpool 8.

Holly derives from an Andy Warhol character in Lou Reeds 'Walk On The Wild Side'.

The band's first three singles reached number one, thus emulating the achievement of another Liverpool band Gerry and the Pacemakers in the 1960's.

Their first record 'Relax' was banned by the BBC but despite this was a world- wide hit record and a must worn tee-shirt.

The group's album 'Liverpool' was released in Autumn 1986.

Holly left the band in 1987 as he was unhappy with the musical direction they were taking. He went solo and enjoyed success including a number one best selling album Blast.

He has continued to make music with his own Pleasuredrome label and since the mid nineties he has worked as a successful painter and has had his works displayed at the Tate in Liverpool and at several galleries in London. In 1994 his autobiography was published 'A bone In My Flute.'

Caption caption caption caption caption
caption caption caption caption caption
caption caption caption caption caption caption

HOLLY JOHNSON

BILLY BUTLER

He is the consumate DJ – a mind packed full of trivia and a knowledge of music that is second-to-none.

Billy was born in North Wales on 25 January 1942 at Salem Street, Amlwch, Anglesey. This was to escape the heavy bombing. His father Frank was a heavy goods driver and died in 1954. This left his mother Gladys to bring up the family and after their move back to Liverpool they lived in Grey Rock Street off West Derby Road.

Gladys died in 1993. Billy attended Whitefield Road County Primary School off Breck Road and on passing the scholarship, the Liverpool Collegiate Grammar School in Shaw Street.

Known as Mrs B's eldest, he left school in 1958 and worked as a plumber and then as a dock clerk, which entailed him delivering shipping documents to the various consulates and shipping offices in the Pier

GREY ROCK STREET

...key Mrs. A
...son Mrs. Madeline
Parry Ivor
32 Riley E
34 Daly Frank
36 Kenny Jas. T
44 O'Brien Chas
46 Brennan Wm
48 Brooks Leslie
52 Butler Mrs. G
54 Williams E
56 Felton Edwd. J
58 Riozzie Philip Alphor
60 Eyre Saml. Edwd
62 Myers Rt
64 O'Hagan Andrew
66 Hughes Danl
68 McKinley Alan

Head area including the Custom House in the Cunard building.

He came to national attention in the entertainment world when he made regular appearances in the early 1960's on the pop music TV programme'

Thank Your Lucky Stars '.

Billy is best remembered on this show for his large comb whilst Janice Nichols from the Birmingham area who worked alongside him, used to utter the immortal words ' I'll give it foive '

He sang briefly with the Merseybeats and then formed his own band The Tuxedos.

He was also DJ at the Cavern Club for five years replacing the legendary Bob Wooler, as well as at a number of different venues including The Mardi Gras, 19 Mount Pleasant and the Downbeat at 77 Victoria Street and in the 1970's at the She Club also in the same street.

He was a regular columnist for the Liverpool Echo and has appeared on both national TV and Radio in the 1980's presenting his own programmes.

A lynchpin of local radio he has broadcast on the local airways since 1971 for both Radio Merseyside and Radio City. 'Hold Your Plums' which he presented with Wally Scott became so popular that its fame extended far beyond the Merseyside boundary.

He is currently in his third spell at Radio Merseyside and continues to attract high audience figures.

He married his second wife Leslie on 10 August 1991 at St James Church in New Brighton and the couple live in the popular Merseyside seaside resort. His first marriage in 1964 to Carol ended in divorce. The couple have four sons Stewart, Lee, David and Paul.

Billy is an avid Everton FC supporter and in the seventies was the match day announcer at Goodison Park.

Pilot of the airwaves-Billy Butler (opposite) on his popular BBC Merseyside show and (right) with Hold Your Plums co-star Wally scott.

RODNEY STREEET

The 'Harley' Street of Liverpool

A true street star of Liverpool. Elegant, sophisiticated home to doctors, dentists, specialists and artistsic types. Birthplace of William Gladstone.

Rodney Street has been seen as abackdrop in many TV dramas. A place that has lost none of its charm – situated amid a thriving tourist area.

RODNEY
STREEET

KENNETH
COPE

He's an actor who excels in playing loveable characters. He starred in Coronation Street and Brookside, but is best remembered as ghost Marty Hopkirk in Randall and Hopkirk (Deceased).

Kenneth was born on 14 April 1931 in the Wavertree district of Liverpool to John and Mary Cope. The family home was at 37 Eastdale Road. He attended Hey Green Road Primary School and then Old Swan Technical College in Broadgreen Road. On leaving school he joined his father who worked at the Automatic Telephone Company in Edge Lane, as an apprentice engineer. With his good friend Norman Rossington, Ken was a member of the 10th Wavertree Scout Troup and appeared in many gang shows. It was whilst in the scouts that he learned to play the trumpet to a very good standard. At one gang show production he so impressed that he was invited to join a new company at the David Lewis Theatre group in Great George Place and eventually he was given a grant from the Liverpool Education Committee to study at the Bristol Old Vic Theatre School. Ken would later say that he owes a good deal to Eric Beaumont his scoutmaster who encouraged him in his desire to become an actor. He left Liverpool at the age of nineteen and married actress Renny Lister in August 1964. The couple have three children, Mark born in 1966, Nicholas 1967 and Martha in 1970. Mark and Nicholas were members of the group The Candyskins and Martha is also an actress. Kenneth is best known for his portrayal of Marty Hopkirk in the television series 'Randall and Hopkirk Deceased' which ran for fourteen months and 26 episodes. He is also remembered as Jed Stone in the early days of Coronation Street and it was here that he met his wife when they appeared together in the long running soap. In later years they have worked together in the restaurant business in Oxford where they both live. A dedicated Everton supporter Ken returns to Liverpool whenever he can to watch his beloved blues.

Coping with fame – a young Kenneth Cope (opposite) in the 60s and (below) enjoying fame as Jed Stone in Coronation Street

EASTDALE ROAD

...nas
..s Thos
...er Fredk
...chbridge Mrs. F
...icDermott Mrs. M
...Bolton Rt
.9 Thomas Wltr. J
31 Hobson Jack
33 Ward Edwd
35 Riley Philip Chas
37 Cope Jn. charge hand
39 Green Mrs. Eliz
41 Houghton Mrs
43 Bertwistle Randolph
45 Parkinson Mrs. M
47 Radcliffe Fredk
49 Parry Mrs. E
51 Eborall Jn. Hy
53 Dennick Regnld

SIMON RATTLE

Simon Rattle was the child prodigy who became one of the most respected and sought after conductors in the world.

The family home was at 13 Menlove Avenue close to Queens Drive. Simon's father Denis was a company director who later trained as an English teacher. He had met his wife Pauline Greening in Dover, where she ran a music shop. Denis also taught the guitar and piano and was a frequent visitor to Paulines shop. They married in 1941 and shortly afterwards moved to Liverpool. Their first child Susan was born in 1946, Simon following some nine years later on 19 January 1955. For many years Susan has worked as a librarian at the Picton library in the city centre. A child prodigy, Simon developed an interest in music from an early age, and at just six years made his public debut at a concert at the Bluecoat School in Church Road. He attended Newborough Preparatory School and then Liverpool College where, like the other boys, he listened to the Beatles and the Rolling Stones etc. Simon was entranced by classical music and in particular Mahler. He was now a proficient percussionist and pianist and a member of the Merseyside Youth Orchestra. In 1966 at the age of eleven he won an Education Authority music scholarship and the

LEFT SIDE.
...as. Mutrie, L.D.S.R.C.
...dental surgn. (surgery)
...J., L.D.S. dental surgn
...yland J. J. D., L.D.S.R.C.
    dental surgn
...Leyland Mary F., M.B., Ch.
    physcn. and surgn
5 Procter Arth. G
7 Helme Mrs. J
9 Loader Edwd. B
11 Wake B
13 Rattle Denis G

Queen's drive

15 Jackson Percvl. Jn
17 Evans Thos. H
19 Ferrigno G
21 Wolfson Mrs. M
23 Potter Simeon
25 Grant Miss Frances C

MENLOVE AVENUE

following year was named Liverpool Music Student of the Year. At the age of sixteen he stood in as a piano soloist with the Merseyside Concert Orchestra at the Philharmonic Hall. Having achieved four top grade A levels he was accepted at the Royal Academy of Music in London where he excelled. He has conducted most of the leading orchestras in the world including the Berlin Philharmonic and the Los Angeles Symphony Orchestra. He also was the conductor of the City of Birmingham Symphony Orchestra for 20 years. He is undoubtedly one of the leading conductors in the world a fact recognised by numerous awards including the CBE and a knighthood for his services to music. Since 2003 he has been the conductor of the Berlin Philharmonic Orchestra regarded by many as the finest in the world. In 2006 he was made an Honorary Fellow of the Society of Arts. On 4 September 2008 he performed at the Philharmonic Hall with his Berlin Orchestra. Twice married, he now lives with his partner the Czech soprano Magdelena Kozena to whom he has a son Jonas. He also has two sons from his first marriage to the American Soprano singer Elise Ross.

Classical act. Simon Rattle (opposite) and above in relaxed mode.

BILL KENWRIGHT

Bill Kenwright is an impresario, true blue Evertonian and one-time TV and pop music heart-throb. Bill has kept many theatrical and sporting careers alive on stage and on the pitch with his respective passions.

...h solctr
Anne
Mrs. E
...P
...d Rd
...terhouse Jas
...ker Bert A
...illiams Leslie B
...Norris Geo. Saml., A.C.A. accntnt
...2 Ashton Isaac J
...04 Deacon Abraham

Storrsdale rd
Greenhill rd

MATHER AVENUE

106 Kenwright Albt
108 Stephens Clifford
110 Watson Mrs. Irene
112 Phillips Jsph
114 Moore Chas. H
116 Gudge Laurence
118 Newman Hyman

Bill was born on 4 September 1945 to Albert and Hope (nee Jones) Kenwright, and lived in Mather Avenue in the Allerton area of Liverpool.

He attended Booker Avenue County Primary School and on passing the scholarship, from March 1957 the Liverpool Institute High School in Mount Street at the same time as George Harrison and Paul McCartney and newscaster Peter Sissons.

Whilst at the Institute (Now LIPA) he appeared in several school plays including playing the part of Shylock in The Merchant Of Venice.

He was also the treasurer of the Christian Union. He left the Institute in 1963.

He had no formal acting training and somewhat stumbled into the profession.

Early parts included that of Gordon Clegg the illegitimate son of Betty Turpin in Coronation Street, and appearances in Z Cars the 1960s BBC television police drama series set in the fictional Newtown but really based on life in Kirkby.

It is ironic that his beloved Everton Football Club adopted the theme music of Z Cars as their signature tune and may be moving from Goodison Park to a new ground in Kirkby.

A lifelong Evertonian, Bill became Chairman of the club in 2004 after serving as a director and Vice Chairman for several years. He began watching Everton in the mid fifties and his hero was the fiery centre forward Dave Hickson.

In later years Bill and Dave have become good friends and in 1999 Bill organised a surprise 70th birthday party for Dave which was based on a 'This Is Your Life' theme when Dave was reunited with former friends and players, many of whom he had not seen for years. Bill was also responsible for Dave's position as a match day greeter in the hospitality lounge at Goodison Park.

Bill is a successful Theatrical Producer and is probably best known for producing the smash hit 'Blood Brothers' which he took to New York.

In 2000 he was awarded the CBE for his services to film and the theatre and in 2001 the KBE.

He also has his own record label(Bill Kenwright Records) and as of 2008 had three albums released including the debut release of his own band Dream On. He has lived in London for many years but is a regular visitor to Liverpool due to his Everton commitments, and also to visit his family.

Hands on theatre guru Bill Kenwright (opposite) and at a dress rehearsal (left) and smiling at a good review of one of his shows

FREDDIE STARR

Freddie Starr is a show biz survivor from his natural comedy antics as a child to pop star, stand-up comedian, TV and film star. He tours regularly. A Scouser you simply can't put down .. just try.

WHARNCLIFFE ROAD

David canvasser
William cycle mech
Doric
adon Gilbt. postman
Robb Edgar Wm. butcher
Jones Thos. Albt. corporati
ployee
41 Fitzgerald Patrick signalman
43 Sunners Jn. Edwd. insur. ag
45 Jones Wm. Emlyn wireman
53 Mahou Mrs
55 Bishop Jn. Thos
57 Stewart Frederick hospital p
59 Bailey Mrs. Jessie
61 Fowell Geo. Hy. bricklyr
63 Thompson Mrs. Helena
65 Drohan Jn. Jas. engine drive
67 Humphreys Edwd. Hy. engn
69 Gill Jn
71 Ambrose Mrs. Margt. Annie
73 Cain Miss Ann
75 Harris Jph. motor driver

Born Frederick Leslie Fowell on 9 January 1943 at 61 Wharncliffe Road Old Swan, he went to Secondary School in Huyton where he developed a talent for impersonating teachers,for which he is remembered more than any academic prowess.

At the age of 14 he had a bit part as a young hoodlum in the film 'The Violent Playground' which was based in Liverpool and also featured Stanley Baker and Anne Heywood. His father George was a bricklayer, and Freddie on leaving school also worked on several building sites, and for a short while as a furniture salesman.

He also tried his hand at boxing a skill he had probably learned from his father who was a bare knuckle fighter. Show business though was always his main ambition and he sang with his backing group the Midnighters and later the Delmonts having now adopted the stage name Freddie Starr. In 1961 he had joined Howie Casey and the Seniors who were the first Mersey band to make a record in Britain with 'Double Twist' on the Fontana label.

He trod the same boards as numerous Liverpool groups including the Beatles playing at the Cavern Club and at the Star Club in Hamburg. In 1970 he moved with his wife and son to live in Woodchurch Road, Birkenhead but the marriage broke up shortly afterwards.

By now he was enjoying a successful solo career as a comedian specialising in impersonations and also as a singer. 1974 saw him reach number nine in the UK single charts with 'It's You'.

In the 1980s his career suffered something of a downward spiral due mainly to financial difficulties. He had lost a lot of money in a multi million pound property speculation in Spain and he also accused his manager John Stewart, who came from Dovecot of assaulting him and a court case ensued.

Freddie considered retiring from show business but bounced back and continued to entertain audiences with his zany impressions and off beat humour.

In 1999 he was involved in a serious car accident on the M4 but made a full recovery. He is still touring theatres across the United Kingdom. In 2008 he celebrates 50 years in show business and still recording.

Freddie Starr a fanatical Evertonian freddie (opposite) and on stage in New Brighton (below)

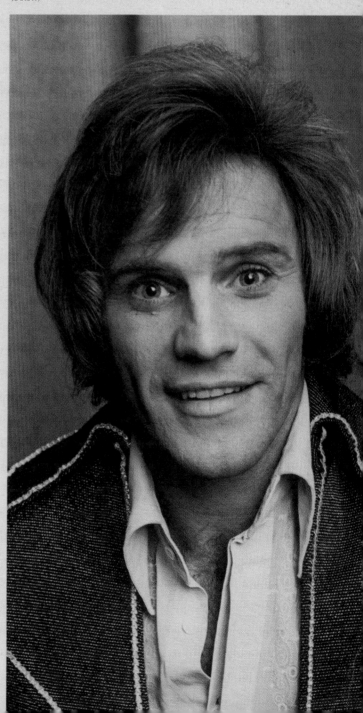

PAULINE COLLINS

A TV star and later a Shirley Valentine, Pauline Collins is a one-woman show.

The family home was firstly in Childwall and then at Radnor Drive in Wallasey. Her Aunt, Grandfather, and other members of the extended family also resided in the large house in Radnor Drive. Pauline was born on 3 September 1940 and was educated locally at the Maris Stella Convent Grammar School in Rowson Street, New Brighton from 1950 to 1952. However Pauline spent much of her time especially weekends at her grandmother's home at 189 Molyneux Road off Sheil Road, Liverpool 6 . For most of the war years the family lived away from Merseyside and although her father was the tenant at Radnor Drive the council decided that he was not there long enough and they were asked to leave in the summer of 1952. She had made many friends in New Brighton and Liverpool and was extremely sad to leave the area. Her father got a teaching job in Battersea and the family moved south with Pauline attending a convent school in Hammersmith. In 1959 they moved to Worthing and Pauline became a teacher, but acting was her first love and following training at the Central School of Drama and Speech she secured several parts in theatre and television. Best known for her appearances in the TV series ' Upstairs Downstairs ' and her role as ' Shirley Valentine ' she is still in much demand. She played the part of Shirley Valentine in Willy Russell's film of the play commissioned by the Everyman Theatre and premiered in 1986. In 2006 she became only the third actor to appear in the original and the then new series of Dr Who. She also regularly appears in pantomime. Pauline was awarded the OBE in 2001 and lives in London with her husband and fellow actor John Alderton. The couple have three children , Nic, Kate and Rick. Pauline also has a daughter, Louise who was adopted in 1962 and whom she did not meet again until 1986, but with whom she is now in regular contact. Pauline subsequently wrote a book called 'Louise' about their experiences of adoption and their period of separation from each other.

Pauline Collins at home with straight drama (opposite) and critically acclaimed stage and film work.

MOLYNEUX ROAD

.... Frank
...t Thos. hairdrssr
..ones Chas. Wm. barman
Provost Jn. Arth. switchbo
    wireman
183 King Donald

Mallow

185 Barrow Jas. foreman
187 Lomax Mrs. Edith
189 Collins Mrs. Eliz
191 Roberts Jn. joiner
193 Huntley Fredk. Cyprus wirema.
195 Lowdey Miss Ada
197 Colebourn Mrs. Lillian

Maxton

199 Potts Thos
201 Jones David tobacco operative

GEORGE HARRISON

The quiet Beatle was born in Wavertree. Whilst at school George worked Saturday mornings as a delivery boy for E R Hughes Butchers, 27 South Parade in Speke. He later became one of the most influencial people in the world.

George was born 25 February 1943, at 12 Arnold Grove in Wavertree to Louise and Harold Harrison.

The house was a cramped two- up, two-down with an outside lavatory, which they rented for ten shillings a week.

The youngest of four, he had two brothers Harold and Peter and a sister Louise.

On 2 January 1950 the family moved to 25 Upton Green, a new council house in Speke. George's mother,and his father a bus driver and a former steward on White Star Liners had been on the Council waiting list for 18 years. This was to be their home until 1 October 1962 when they went to live at 174 Mackets Lane, Hunts Cross. George attended Dovedale Road Primary School and then the Liverpool Institute.

John Lennon was also a pupil at Dovedale Road at the same time as George but as he was two school terms ahead of George it is unlikely that their paths crossed although Peter Harrison was in the same year as John. He would though meet Paul McCartney at the Liverpool Institute although unlike Paul, George was not academic and hated the grammar school environment frittering away his opportunities and failing all his exams.

Whilst at school George worked on Saturday mornings as a delivery boy for E R Hughes Butchers, 27 South Parade in Speke. When he left the Institute in 1959 he was sent by the Youth Employment Service to Blacklers store in Great Charlotte Street were he was taken on as a trainee electrician. It was his job to clean the lights and at Christmas keep the grotto clean. He left Blacklers in August 1960 when the Silver Beatles embarked on their first tour of Hamburg. When the Beatles soared to worldwide fame the Harrisons found it impossible to continue living in Macketts Lane as the house was constantly besieged by fans and finally in 1965 George's father quit his job as a bus driver and he and his wife moved to the village of Appleton near Warrington to a bungalow bought for them by George. Tragically his mother Louise was to spend just five years there dying of a brain tumour on 7 July 1970.

Harold Harrison, a heavy smoker throughout his life, died of emphysema in May 1978. Both parents had been very supportive of George particularly in the early stages of his career.

His mother would personally reply to each fan's letter received at the home. George Harrison sadly passed away on November 2001. A world mourned.

Above: 12 Arnold Grove, Wavertree. The name Arnold belonged to the personal dresser to Queen Victoria.

UPTON GREEN

...hald
...Mrs. L
...eeney Jn
...rayson Geo
...Lenny Arth
20 Spencer Edwd
21 Jackson Mrs. Ellen
22 Naylor Jn. C
23 Ball Mrs. G
24 Childs Jn
25 Harrison Harold
26 Proudfoot Gordon
27 Cobourne Percy
28 Jones Alfd. E
29 McDonnell Jn
30 McGovern Danl
31 Cubley Norman

UPTON PARK DRIVE, UPTON,
BIRKENHEAD. 102 *Manor drive.*
[Letters should be addressed Wirral,
Cheshire.]

The 'Quiet'one - the spiritual Beatle was fond of Arnold Grove which still stands to this day in Wavertree. It's a place he mentioned with great affection in his wonderfully witty autobiography called I Me Mine!

But of all The Beatles George was the one who did not seem to mention the importance of being from Liverpool that often.

He retained a great sense of humour and a distinctive accent which he had till the day he died.

George, the nworking class son of a bus conductor, did return to the city with his second wife, Olivia to see the neat two-up and two-down home not far from the Picton Clock and the Abbey Cinema.

To this day a family live there and do not seem to mind the daily visits from coach loads of fans on the Magical Mystery coach tours.

Some are so taken abackwith the ordinariness of this humble birthplace that they kiss the door where Beatle George spent a part of his early life.

On the last visit to the city in the 90s, George and Olivia called in to Mathew Street and he even popped into The Beatle Shop.He then asked a fellow shopper where was the best place to have a drink? And then went into the Crocodile Pub sporting a long beard and coat – he was suitably disguised.

George, who lived in Oxfordshire, once said that he would rather have been a gardener than a Beatle and it was a substantial cheque from him that helped save the Victorian Palm House in Sefton Park. George once said that "we are all just water and molecules here on a visit."

But what a visit… from Arnold Grove to global success he, also once said matter-of-factly in his Scouse accent: "The Beatles saved the world from boredom."

While his guitar gently smiled (opposite) . Here comes the sunflower for gardener George (right).

JIMMY TARBUCK

He is the gap-toothed comic with his catchphrase 'boom boom'. Jimmy Tarbuck was once described as 'the Motop comedian.'

Jimmy was born at Sefton General Hospital on 6 February 1940 to Fred and Frances Tarbuck.

He has a sister Norma and a brother Ken.Sadly, another brother Freddie died when young.

Jimmy's father was a bookmaker with premises at 170a London Road whilst his mother known as Fanny appeared on the stage for a number of years.

The family home was at 74 Queens Drive, Mossley Hill and the young Jimmy attended Dovedale Road, Primary School at the same time as John Lennon and George Harrison.

Jimmy recalls going on a school camping trip to the Isle of Man organised by Mr Fred Bolt which John also attended.

He was also in the same class as Georges elder brother Peter. Jimmy passed the scholarship and was transferred to St Francis Xavier Grammar school, Beaconsfield Lane, Woolton but was expelled for persistent truanting and general bad behaviour.

He finished his school days at Rose Lane Secondary Modern in Allerton.

On leaving school he had a variety of jobs including butchers boy, working in a laundry, apprentice car mechanic, TV Salesman and as an apprentice hairdresser at Andre Bernard, Ranelagh Street.

His break into show business occurred when he was on holiday at Butlins in Pwhelli with his friends the Liverpool footballers Jimmy Melia, Bobby Campbell and Johnny Morrisey.

They urged him to take part in a talent competition which he won and he went on to make his professional debut in a Rock and Roll tour which starred Marty Wilde and which featured another young Liverpudlian. Bill Fury.

Jimmy was a promising young footballer who had trials with his beloved Liverpool and played at a reasonable level in the Welsh league.

He married Pauline Carfoot of 91 Cockburn Street, Liverpool 8 whom he had met at a fair, and with whom he spent a lot of time at the famous Cavern Club.

The couple have three chidren Cheryl born in 1962, Liza in 1966 and James born in 1969. Liza of course went on to become a star in her own right. Jimmy and Pauline now live in Surrey but Jimmy visits Liverpool whenever he can particularly Anfield to watch Liverpool FC. He was also a frequent visitor to his parent's home who had moved in the late 1960's to Warren Drive in New Brighton. He was awarded the OBE in 1994 for his services to show business and charity.

One of the nation's great quiz show hosts (oposite) and iback in liverpool for the Royal Variety Show.

QUEENS DRIVE

Menlove av
Allerton rd

Culligan Mrs. Grace
8 Shennan Mrs. Olga
68 Johnson Vernon School of Dance & Drama
72 Charrick Bernard
74 Tarbuck Fred
76 Roberts Rt. R
78 Lipkin Mrs. Evelyn
80 Wilkinson Edwd. Blair, M.B. Ch.B. physcn. and surgn
82 Bell J. Fraser, B.D.S.L'pool dental surgn
84 Zucker Mrs. D. C
Williams Pearce

ALAN BLEASDALE

Alan Bleasdale started out with a fear of flying but soon went on to soar as one of Liverpool's most prolific award-winning and generous of writers who still nurtures new talent.

With his trusty typewriter (opposite) and above on the streets he loves during Boys From The Blackstuff.

Alan an only child was born 23 March 1946 to George and Margaret Bleasdale. The family lived at 40 Liverpool Road in Huyton close to the Farmers Arms Public House.

His father was a strong disciplinarian his mother suffered from several phobias some of which have been inherited by Alan.

He particularly had a fear of flying and did not step on a plane until 2006 when his youngest son got married in the U.S.A.

He attended St Aloysius Junior School in Twig Lane and from 1957 to 1964 Wade Deacon Grammar School, Birchfield Road, Widnes.

A keen Liverpool FC supporter he was on their books for a short while and failed to make the grade but played amateur football to a reasonable standard. He trained to be a teacher at Padgate College in Warrington which later became Warrington Collegiate Institute, and obtained his teaching certificate in 1967.

In 1970 he married Julia Moses. The couple have two sons and one daughter all now in their thirties. Alan taught at St Columbas Secondary Modern School in Hillside Road, Huyton for eight years and then King George V School also in Huyton, which he left in 1975.

His final teaching post was at Halewood Grange Comprehensive School. For a while he had attempted to combine his teaching duties with his play writing but eventually he had to go full time.

He also worked for a brief period in 1970 as a part-time security guard at the docks. From 1975 to 1986 he worked as a playwright at the Liverpool Playhouse becoming associate director. In the mid seventies to the early eighties he lived with his young family at 97 Elm Vale near Newsham Park.

In 1971 he had created Franny Scully a character loosely based on his own childhood experiences and which was first broadcast on Radio Merseyside. He has since written numerous productions too many to mention in full with perhaps 'Boys from the Blackstuff' being the best known. He also penned The Monocled Mutineer and G.B.H. Most of his work is inspired by his own personal experiences and life in Liverpool. He has been awarded several honours for his writing and producing, including a BAFTA and best TV drama series.

His contribution to the arts in Liverpool and in particular the Playhouse Theatre, to whom he is always indebted for giving him his big break is incalculable. He still lives in the city.

LIVERPOOL ROAD

Mrs. Ellen
...aw Jn. E
...Cooper Wm. Hy. bldr
20 Male Sydney
22 Taylor Stanley
24 Hewitt Misses S. & E
    "Farmers' Arms" P
        McChrystal
40 **Bleasdale Geo**
42 Preston Mrs. Gertrude
44 Brennan Jas. Timothy co
46 Kirkham Harry E. forem
48 Fletcher Jn. Alex. plumb
        Path to Wool
Methodist Church
County Council School
    Child Welfare Associa
66 Haswell Chas. confctnr

...gh rd

A Street star is born again, Bold Street, the grand old lady of constant change – is the city's equivalent of London's Bond Street. Close your eyes and you can imagine the horse- drawn carriages moving along.

BOLD STREET

Alberto Remedios – one of the greatest tenors Liverpool has ever produced. The Sadler's Wells star was greatly influenced by fellow Scouser and opera diva, Rita Hunter.

Alberto owes his name to a Spanish immigrant grandfather. He was born on 27 February 1935, at 166 Grove Street, Liverpool 8.

His parents Albert and Ida loved opera and the family home resounded to recordings of Caruso and the other great singers of the day. Alberto attended St Margaret's School in Upper Hampton Street off Princes Road.

At the age of seven he joined the choir of St Saviour's Parish Church in Falkner Square.

On leaving school he worked as an apprentice welder at Cammell Laird's shipyard in Birkenhead.

An excellent young footballer he played for New Brighton FC as a semi-professional until injury curtailed his career. He has remained over the years an enthusiastic supporter of Liverpool FC and Bill Shankly was one of the guests when Alberto was featured on " This is Your Life ".

Singing, though, was his main love and he received voice training from Edwin Francis who had premises at Byrom's Studios at 27 Houghton Street, Liverpool 1.

He was recognised as one of the country's foremost teachers of singing.

Alberto was also greatly influenced by fellow pupil Rita Hunter who lived in Wallasey and with whom he developed a life long friendship. She went on to achieve international fame as an operatic singer.

Alberto commenced singing in local clubs and once shared a bill with Ken Dodd.

After completing his two years National Service he joined the Sadler's Wells Opera in 1956 and in 1958 he won the Queen's Prize for the best young opera singer in the country. The same year he married Shirley Swindells who lived at 42 Langdale Road, Wavertree at St Bridget's Church in Bagot Street.

Many more awards followed and in 1981 he was awarded the CBE.

He was once described by one critic as what Bobby Moore the ex England football captain is to football, Alberto Remedios is to opera, a master of his trade, cool and unflappable. Praise indeed! His rich tenor tones have been heard in many of the world's great opera houses.

Latterly he has lived in semi retirement in Australia. His younger brother Ramon born 9 May 1940 also a tenor followed in his operatic footsteps without quite achieving the high standards of Alberto.

Albert on stage in Italy and out of costume,
Opposite The 'Bobby Moore' of Opera.
A voice that spoke and sang volumes.

GROVE STREET

148 Pilnick David
160 Flanagan Jn
162 House of Help (Miss
    Stace matron)
164 Randle Peter Oliver, M.R.C.,
    veterinary surgn
164 Levin David Arnold, B.A., M.I,
    L'pool physcn
166 Remedios Albt
168 Gantoa Emmanuel
170 Tahir Husin Ben
172 Mass Miss Fanny
174 Coleman Mrs. Bridget Mary
178 Brogan Philip
              Falkner st
188 Riley Mrs. Sarah
      Back Falkner street South
194 Fox Thos
              Falkner sq

ALBERTO
REMEDIOS

REX
HARRISON

Rex Harrison was an international star who hailed from Huyton. He epitomised the English 'gent' on stage and screen with his crystal cut accent, manner and charm.

Undoubtedly one of the finest film stars Merseyside and Britain has ever produced. Rex was born in Huyton on 5 March 1908. Christened Reginald, the youngest of three children, the family home was at Derry House on Tarbock Road, an imposing dwelling in keeping with the other residences in the vicinity. There was money on his father Williams side of the family. Their previous residence had been the imposing Belle Vale Mansion, but his father's bankruptcy meant it had to be sold. Today the area is covered with the houses of the Belle Vale estate. His father was a trained engineer but took a career at the Stock Exchange in Imperial Buildings, Exchange Street. He was an excellent hockey player and was a member of the West Derby Hockey Club and won an England cap. Reginald's early schooling was in Huyton but at the onset of the First World War the family moved to Sheffield and it was here that he decided to call himself Rex apparently realising that it is the Latin name for King. His fathers work brought him back to Liverpool, the family taking up residency firstly at 5 Lancaster Avenue near Sefton Park and then at nearby 110 Hartington Road. Rex was now a pupil at Liverpool College and in Howson's House where his drama skills were soon evident, with him appearing in numerous school productions which in turn opened the door to appearances at the Crane Theatre in Hanover Street and at the Playhouse. He missed a lot of schooling due to ill health and years later it was found that he had been suffering from tuberculosis which managed to right itself. He also had poor eyesight and in his early days wore a monocle which cut quite a sight particularly on his regular visits to the Adelphi Hotel. He made his professional stage debut for the Liverpool Rep in 1924 in a play titled 'Thirty Minutes In A Street '. London eventually called and he severed his physical ties with Merseyside. He will probably be best remembered for his role as Professor Higgins in 'My Fair Lady' for which he won an Oscar in 1964. Despite his internationally renowned stardom he however never forgot his Merseyside roots and would often reminisce about his time at Liverpool College. Dubbed 'Sexy Rexy' no doubt due to his renowned womanising and his six marriages Sir Reginald Carey Harrison died in Manhattan on 2 June 1990 at the age of 82.

Rex in a classical role (opposite) in My Fair Lady and 'sexy Rexie' during Hollywood film promotion (above).

Rev. Christphr., M.A. (Methodist)
Williams Thos. representative
Sieve Michl. credit draper
96 Sieve Mrs. Bluma
98 Levy Mrs. Annie
100 Garrett Mrs. Lavinia
102 Myer Myers mfrs.' agt
102 Levy Simon
104 Moore Mrs. Eliz. victualler
Croxteth grove
106 Nicolaides Mrs. D
106 Fayle Percy stationer
108 Beakbane Miss Florence,O.B.E.,J.P
110 Harrison Wm. Reginld
Croxteth road

HARTINGTON ROAD, GARSTON (19)
5 Clarendon road
RIGHT SIDE.
2 Richards Mrs. Irene
4 Rigby J. W. & Son (Garston) Ltd

HARTINGTON ROAD

BERYL
BAINBRIDGE

Beryl Bainbridge, author. A regular voice in the newspapers, she has an opinion about most subjects. Outspoken Beryl is the author of the brilliant novel 'Young Adolf'.

Beryl was born not far from Crosby on 21 November 1932.

Her father Richard, who was born in 1889, served as a cabin boy sailing from Liverpool to New York.

He worked in the Cotton Exchange in Old Hall Street but was made bankrupt in 1929 and was later employed as a salesman.

Beryl experienced an unhappy childhood and witnessed frequent arguments between her parents mainly over money matters. She attended Merchant Taylors' College for Girls in Crosby.

When she was fourteen her mother Winifred discovered a suggestive ditty in Beryl's pocket and took it to the headmistress and she was promptly expelled. As no other school in the area would accept her she attended a ballet school in Manchester which she loved, having commenced dancing at the age of six the time she also started writing.

She then obtained work at the Liverpool Playhouse and It was here that she met a young student, Austin Davies, who painted some of the scenery at the theatre.The couple married and had two children.

He would later teach both John Lennon and Stuart Sutcliffe at the Liverpool College of Art.

They lived for a while in a flat in Huskisson Street and divorced in 1959 but remained friends. Both were regulars at the 23 club in Hope Street which was a meeting place for local writers and artists.

She moved to London in 1963 and has lived there ever since.

A keen writer she first kept a diary, most of Beryl's work is loosely based on her unhappy childhood experiences.

One of her most popular novels' Young Adolf' published in 1978,is based on the fascinating possibility that the young Hitler stayed with his relatives in Liverpool from November 1912 until April 1913.

What is not in question is that his half brother Alois and his wife Bridget Dowling resided at 102 Upper Stanhope Street (see below) with Bridget's father William.

Beryl Bainbridge is an enigmatic figure in Liverpool, who whilst retaining a fondness for the city is not slow to voice her criticisms of what she perceives as its downsides.She did not have anything to do with the Capital of Culture festivities during 2008. She once predicted she would die at the age of 71.

 She didn't.

Author of 'Young Adolf'(oppsite): Young Beryl(above)

UPPER STANHOPE STREET

Margaret
avid Henry foreman
es Robert B.dental mechanic
wards Miss Eunice tchr. of music
vine Mrs. Catherine
Williams Daniel warehouseman
8 Pearson Philip William engineer
90 Higgins Albert decorator
92 Booth Ralph Cedric mariner
94 Almond Thomas horsekeeper
96 Ribton Mrs. Margaret
98 Parry Mrs. Margaret
100 Buchanan John
102 Dowling William

Berkley st

106 Johnson Henry Woollam
108 Taylor Mrs. Mary fancy draper
110 Sablick John bootmaker
112 Merricks Henry & Son upholsterers
114 Milne Alexander provision dealer
116 Lacy William
118 "Prince's Park" P.H.   Michael

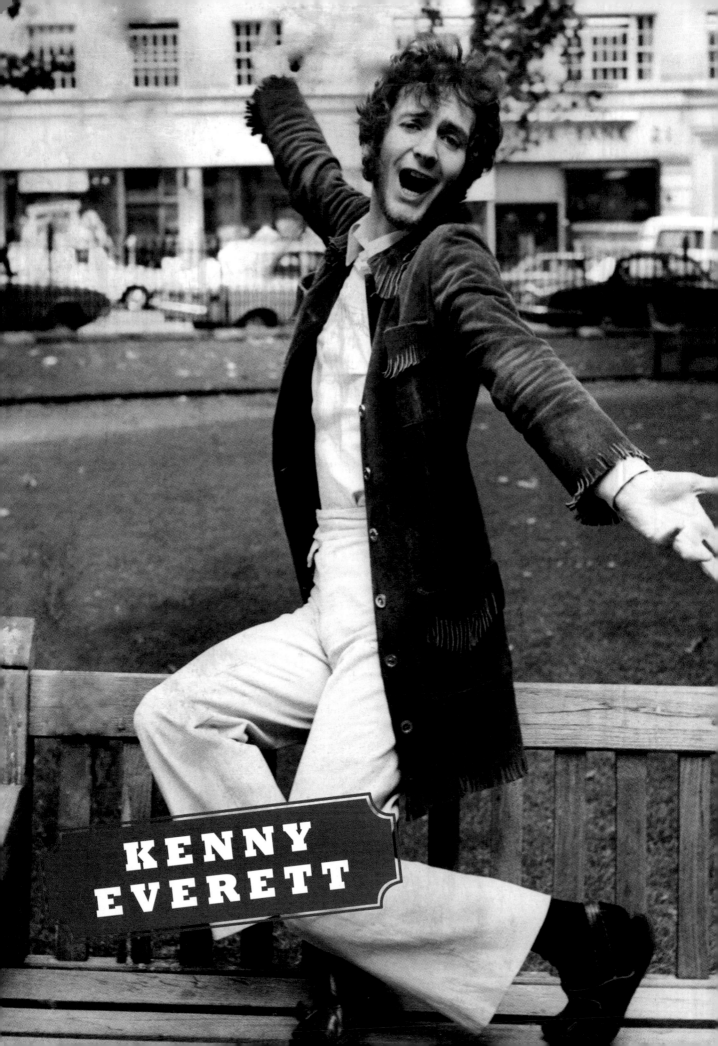

KENNY
EVERETT

Kenny Everett was a mould-breaking DJ who also revolutionised comedy shows. Kenny was a visionary who helped Freddie Mercury and Queen, amongst many others become stars.

Maurice James Christopher Cole was born in 1944 at 14 Hereford Road in Seaforth to Tom, a tugboat skipper and Lil, a shopworker. He had a sister Cathy who was two years older. A studious and religious child he was educated at St Edmunds Primary School, Oxford Road, Waterloo and then St Bede's, Myers Road East in Crosby, and much of his early life was spent attending Mass at St Thomas of Canterbury Church, Great Georges Road, Waterloo. At the age of 13 he transferred to Stillington Hall School near York with a view to later ordination to the Priesthood but after two years he was expelled and returned to St Bede's. Much of his childhood was spent on his own and he enjoyed trips on the overhead railway or on the ferry boat to New Brighton. His first job on leaving school was at Coopers Bakery and then at Albert Douglass and Co Ltd an advertising agency at 15 Tithebarn Street. Finally he was advertising manager for the Journal of Commerce and Shipping Telegraph, 17 James Street near the Pierhead. His break into show business, and his remarkable personality change from a somewhat introverted character to the zany performer he became, occurred almost overnight. His big opening came when he was recruited by Radio London having sent them some tapes which they were impressed with and promptly recruited him. He was sent by Radio London to the U.S.A in 1964 to cover the Beatles tour and the Americans were fascinated by somebody from the Beatles home city who had actually seen them perform at the Cavern Club. By now he had changed his name to Kenny Everett and became well known nationally for the popular TV programme ' The Kenny Everett Video Show'. He chose the name Everett from the film star Edward Everett Horton one of his childhood heroes. Having been diagnosed as HIV positive in 1986 he died in 1995 aged just fifty one. Sadly he never seemed to come to terms with his sexuality and suffered from bouts of depression after coming out in 1979. Following his death his family donated his private studio where he created much of his radio work to LIPA, to encourage the young people of Merseyside to follow in Kenny's creative footsteps.

King Kenny, aka Cuddly Ken,- the much-loved Liverpool DJ who inspired many household names (opposite) above larking around in his recording studio at home.

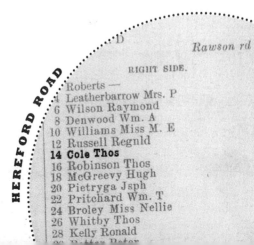

HEREFORD ROAD

RIGHT SIDE.

Rawson rd

	Roberts —
4	Leatherbarrow Mrs. P
6	Wilson Raymond
8	Denwood Wm. A
10	Williams Miss M. E
12	Russell Regnld
14	**Cole Thos**
16	Robinson Thos
18	McGreevy Hugh
20	Pietryga Jsph
22	Pritchard Wm. T
24	Broley Miss Nellie
26	Whitby Thos
28	Kelly Ronald

PETER PRICE

Pete Price stand-up, award-winning broadcaster, newspaper columnist now author. 'I'll knock you out,' is his catchphrase."

Peter Lloyd Price was born in March 1946 and adopted at the age of two months. The family home was in Grainger Avenue, West Kirby and after failing the eleven plus examination he attended Hoylake Parade Secondary Modern School where he became proficient in cookery. Shortly after leaving school he secured a job as a cook on a cruise ship where he also did some entertaining. He joined the fledgling BBC Radio Merseyside as a DJ at the age of 21 and since then has rarely been off the local airwaves. He has also worked at Radio One, had a regular column in the Liverpool Echo, and for a number of years was the resident compere at the Shakespeare Club in Fraser Street. He currently hosts a late night call show at Radio City which has not been without incident, including an occasion in 2006 when one of his regular telephone callers went quiet on air. Peter rushed to the man's home to find an ambulance present, the caller having died of a heart attack.

Openly gay Peter came out to his mother at the age of 19 who believing he was ill referred him to a GP who had him admitted to a psychiatric hospital in Chester were he spent three days receiving aversion therapy, which included injections, causing a violent reaction. He would later describe the experience as the worst three days of his life. He made contact with his biological mother in 1997 and discovered that his father was a POW from Sicily, whom his mother had met when she worked at an internment camp in Warrington towards the end of World War Two. All attempts to trace his father through the official channels, including the Italian Embassy, failed so he enlisted the help of the Mafia in Sicily which has so far proved unsuccessful. Peter's contribution to Merseyside entertainment is immeasurable and he also works tirelessly for many local charities including Claire House where he is a patron.

Pete dealing with his late night audience of winners and losers (opposite). Above during a promotion campaign for his best-selling autobiography – Namedropper.

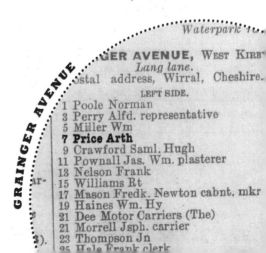

GRAINGER AVENUE

GER AVENUE, WEST KIRB*
Lang lane.
ostal address, Wirral, Cheshire.

LEFT SIDE.
1 Poole Norman
3 Perry Alfd. representative
5 Miller Wm
7 **Price Arth**
9 Crawford Saml. Hugh
11 Pownall Jas. Wm. plasterer
13 Nelson Frank
15 Williams Rt
17 Mason Fredk. Newton cabnt. mkr
19 Haines Wm. Hy
21 Dee Motor Carriers (The)
21 Morrell Jsph. carrier
23 Thompson Jn
25 Hole Frank clerk

Waterpark

MALANDRA
BURROWS

From child star to household favourite Malandra Burrows has a golden smile and a personality to match.

Born Malandra Elizabeth Burrows in Woolton on 4 November 1965, her Christian name is a portmanteau of her parent's names Malcolm and Sandra. She is the eldest child of three, her sister Starrianna is two years younger and her brother Shawn six years younger. The family lived in Charterhouse Road and then Monica Road in Woolton. A child star she appeared on TV's ' Junior Showtime' at the age of six having commenced dancing lessons when just two. All three children were performing at a young age as a trio singing and dancing. At the age of eleven Malandra became the youngest ever winner of the popular television talent show ' New Faces ' and at thirteen was BBC Radio Merseyside's songwriter of the year. She was a pupil at Woolton County Primary School and then at King David High School in Childwall Road (see below) where she developed an interest in journalism, and at one point was seriously considering it as a career. She has since written weekly columns for a range of provincial newspapers. She left school with nine passes at GCE 'O' Level and joined the Everyman Youth Theatre and Liverpool Theatre School. She was also a member of St Peter's Amateur Dramatic Company in Woolton Village. Early appearances on Brookside were a prelude to her best known role, that of Kathy Merrick (Glover) in the TV soap Emmerdale Farm later to become Emmerdale. She played the part for sixteen years from 1985 to 2001, before departing in somewhat acrimonious circumstances although she has since made occasional guest appearances. A talented singer she reached number eleven in the charts with her 1990 single ' Just The Other Side Of Love '. She is still in much demand as an actress, and keeps in contact with her native city mainly through her support of Liverpool Football Club and family visits. Away from acting she keeps fit by regular visits to the gym and is also a keen runner. In June 2008 her fitness stood her in good stead when she fought back as a car thief attempted to steal her vehicle from outside her West Yorkshire home.

Young Malandra had star quality as a child and proved with with her role later in Emmerdale and I'm a Celebrity Get Me Out of Here.

Geo
McNiven Raymond
47 Ellis Rt
49 Allum Geoffrey
51 Williamson Arth
53 Forsyth Thos
55 Hollywood Thos
59 Jones Wm .
RIGHT SIDE.
4 Amies Rd
6 Lewis Harold
8 Borrows Malcolm R
10 McEvoy Jas
12 Mitchell David A
14 Davies Kenneth
16 Gilbert Wm D
18 Maysmor Dudley
20 Hughes Thos
22 Nolan Jn
24 Hennessy Jas
26 Boyle Edwd
28 Prescott Philip
30 Christopher Hy
32 Smith Alfd N
34 Whitelaw Rd

CHARTERHOUSE ROAD

D SWAN (13).

Charlton pl

LIME
STREET

RITA TUSHINGHAM

One of the many talented Liverpool stars to make her name in film. Rita has never forgotten her roots and her birthplace.

Lovely Rita in the sixties with actress Lyn Redgrave (above)
Ms T with George Harrison and Brian Jones and as she is today (opposite).

...as.
...k. Roger clerk
...son Montague Jn
Page Mo

ASHTON CHAMBERS
(See HACKINS HEY 2.)

ASHTON DRIVE, HUNT'S
(19). *Spoke road.*
RIGHT SIDE.

2 **Tushingham Jn**
4 Bellasis Miss M
6 Strachan Jn
8 Downs Wm. tyre mer
10 Drabble Christphr
16 Bond Norman
18 Paul Alfd. civil engnr
20 Acker Manus Leon
22 Tushingham Mrs. Lilian
24 Leyland Wm. motor driver
Hillfoc

ASHTON DRIVE, WEST K

Rita was born on 14 March 1942, the daughter of John and Enid. One of three children the family home was at 2 Ashton Drive, Hunts Cross. Her father had a grocers shop at 176 Garston Old Road where the young Rita would help out on Saturday mornings with her brothers Colin and Peter. John Ashton was very involved in the local community and was president of the Garston Rotary Club and Woolton Boys Club in Vale Road. He was elected to the city council in 1960 at a by – election following in his own fathers footsteps. He was also a keen football fan and the young Rita was taken along with her brothers to both Anfield and Goodison Park on Saturday afternoons. Rita attended La Sagesse Convent High School in Aigburth Road and was involved in several school plays. She was also a member of St Columba's Presbyterian Church Dramatic Society In Hillfoot Avenue. Further stage training took place at the Shelagh Elliot-Clarke School, 63 Rodney Street. She worked at the Playhouse for two years as assistant manager but also undertook a shorthand typing course in case her stage ambitions failed to materialise. Her acting career really took off in 1961 when she secured a part in the film ' A Taste Of Honey ' when just nineteen years of age which won her the Best Actress Award at the Cannes Film Festival . A family celebration took place on 14 July 1964 when her brother Colin married Rita Farnworth from 68 Holt Hill in Birkenhead. They were married at St Stephen's church in Prenton and with Rita in attendance quite a crowd gathered outside the church .At her peak in the 1960's and 1970's, her career tailed off somewhat in the 1980's but she continues to be given parts and in 1999 she appeared in the Liverpool film ' Swing '. A great friend of Carla Lane she made an appearance in Carla's popular series ' Bread '. Rita played the part of a refined Liverpudlian. She is a prolific fund raiser for several charities particularly Cancer Research. Her daughter Aisha was diagnosed as suffering from breast cancer and they are both involved in giving talks and interviews to raise peoples awareness. Rita divides her time between Germany and London.

Frankie Vaughan was a singer, film star and a tireless charity worker particularly in his role as vice president of the National Association of Boys Clubs.

FRANKIE VAUGHAN

Born Frank Ephraim Abelson on 3 February 1928 the eldest of four, he had three younger sisters Myra, Phyliss and Carol. The family lived at 35 Devon Street off London Road.

His father Isaac was the son of a Russian immigrant and had a furniture business on the corner of Lodge Lane. When Frank was eight years old the family moved to 45 Eversley Street where they stayed for eighteen months before settling at 301 Smithdown Lane.

Frank attended the Liverpool Hebrew School which was sited at 1 Hope Place at the corner with Pilgrim Street. With his father and mother Leah a seamstress at work during the day he spent a lot of time at his grandmother's Mrs Kozaks home who lived at 120 Cranbourne Road in Wavertree.

She used to refer to him as her number one grandson. She took him on outings all over Liverpool including to the museum and art gallery and the Pavilion Theatre in Lodge Lane.

He was also a frequent visitor to the King's Cinema in London Road.

As a youngster Frank was a member of the choir at Princes Road Synagogue. On 1 September 1939, 257 children from the Hebrew School including Frank boarded a train at Central Station and set off for Chester where they were billeted at several houses there.

In 1941 the children of Liverpool upped sticks once again and this time Frank and his sisters were evacuated to Endmoor which is situated between Kendal and Kirby Londsdale.

Later on the family all moved to Lancaster and lived at 25 Moor Lane. It was here that Frank joined Lancaster Boys Club thus commencing a lifelong association with youth work. He attended Lancaster College of Art finishing the course in Leeds.

It was in Leeds that his career in show business went on to reach astonishing heights in theatre and film. He also had 31 hit records including 2 number ones.

His first film was 'These Dangerous Years 'which was shot on location in Liverpool and included the Cast Iron shore were Frank had played many times as a child. The story line was about a soldier who deserts the army and returns to his hometown of Liverpool.

Frankie never forgot his roots and would often return to Liverpool particularly in his role as vice president of the National Association of Boys Clubs for whom he was a tireless fundraiser. He latterly lived in High Wycombe with Stella his wife of 48 years, where he sadly passed away on 17 September 1999.

The Frankie Vaughan archive was donated by his widow to Liverpool John Moores University in 2000.

Paul McCartney has described him as the major Liverpool star.

Mr Moonlight Frankie Vaughan in his trademark pose (opposite).

...ter smallware ce...
Chatswor

SMITHDOWN LANE

...7 "Spekeland Arms" Rt.
Ammundsen
301 Ableson Isaac wardrobe dir
303 Evans Geo. confctnr
305 Manby Jn. H. wood workers' su
307 Post, M. O. & Telephone Call
Telegrams dispatched b:
delivered—Miss M. O'Su
M.B.E. postmistress
311 Watson Geo. Alec butcher
311A Keeley Patrick scrap metal x
313 Midland Bank Ltd. (Smit
Lane branch)—John W
Evans manager
319 Sherry William herbalist
319 Magee Jn. dock labourer
321 Kenyon Jn. fishmngr
323 Hargreaves Wm. fruitr. & gre
Tunnel

PAUL
O'GRADY

Paul O'Grady MBE., has one of the sharpest Scouse accents on TV and stage. He is the self-styled Birkenhead bombsite.

Paul was born on 14 June 1955 into an Irish Catholic family. The home was in Holly Grove, Tranmere, Birkenhead. An intelligent youngster he was educated at Blessed Edmund Campion School, Claughton Village and then St Anselm's Catholic College in Manor Hill, Claughton. He was also a member of the Birkenhead Amateur Boxing club and used to box at school. He has had a life time love of boxing. On leaving school at 18 he worked as an assistant clerk at Liverpool Magistrates Court for a short time and then in the Civil Service. A variety of jobs followed including that of barman at Yates Wine Lodge, at an abattoir, as a woodsman and at a children's home in West Kirby. He moved to London and was employed as a peripatetic Care Officer for Camden Council. He has also worked behind a bar in Manila. A precocious talent his acting career took off when he appeared as an extra in Coronation Street and really began to blossom when he took his mothers maiden name Savage and added Lily to it. The Birkenhead bombshell was born! He first appeared as Lily in a pub in London in 1985. The character was created following a party he had attended on a Chinese ship which was berthed in Liverpool. When he went to work the following day someone remarked 'Oh, there goes Shanghai Lil 'and thereafter he was known as Shanghai Lil. Nationwide fame was achieved aftre much hard work playing clubs. The ' Lily Savage Show ' sealed his fame and fate and was scripted by himself and broadcast by BBC TV. In 2002 he suffered a heart attack and was ordered to rest. This was followed in 2006 by a second more serious attack and he was admitted to intensive care and ordered to stop smoking completely. He has lived for a number of years in the South of England and has a flat in London and a farm in Ashford, Kent. He has one daughter Sharyn who married her childhood friend Philip Mosely at Liverpool Town Hall on 30 July 2005 and gave birth to a son, Abel, in 2006 making Paul a doting grandfather. His Paul O'Grady show is currently broadcast on Channel Four. He was awarded the MBE in the 2008 Queen's Birthday honours list. When informed of the honour he thought it was a 'wind up.' It wasn't.

Paul O'Grady and dog Buster (opposite);
Alter ego Lily Savage (above) now in a
nunnery!.

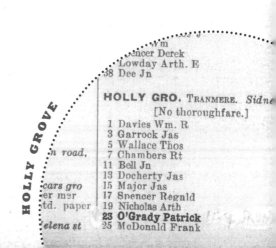

STAN BOARDMAN

Stan 'The Man' Boardman made his stand up name in the holiday camp world and then went on to conquer The London Palladium.

Stan was born in 1937 in the Scotland Road area of the city. The family home was demolished by a bomb in 1942 and they were rehoused in Kirkdale for a short while before settling in Peasefield Road, Dovecot. He was educated firstly at Dovecot County Primary School in Winstone Road and then at Dovecot Secondary Modern School in Grant Road. He left school in 1952 and had a variety of jobs including as a pipe fitter, welder, lifeguard, beach photographer and finally his own haulage business based in Huyton. Stan had

PEASEFIELD ROAD

...ASEFIELD ROAD,
(14). 23 Shellingfor
LEFT SIDE.

1 Holmes Rt. Wm
3 Trainor Fredk
5 Crooks Jn
7 Wilton E
9 Cooper Mrs. Ida
11 Dean Sidney
15 **Boardman Thos**
17 Piper Percy
19 Bresnen Mrs. May
21 Monaghan Thos. Jsph
23 Hardman Jsph. Hy

completed his National Service in the Royal Engineers in 1960. It was while on the dole in the early 1970s and having scraped enough money to take his family on holiday to Butlins Holiday Camp, he was encouraged by his wife and children to enter a talent competition and he won through to the national finals. A late starter on the comedy circuit Stan was in his late thirties when he made his professional debut at Bromborough British Legion Club and was in his forties when he really established himself as a comic having appeared on the popular TV show ' The Comedians ' on ten occasions and then had his own TV show ' The Video Entertainers '. Other Merseyside comics to appear on the Comedians included Paul Melba, Johnny Hackett, George Roper and the first female performer Pauline Daniels. Stan is probably best known for his comments about the Germans which is ironic considering his childhood home in Scotland Road fell victim to a bomb during the Second World War. Stan now lives in the Wirral with his wife Vivienne. They have two children Andrea, a TV Presenter and Paul who was a goalkeeper with Plymouth Argyle and now works for Sky Sports News. A promising player in his younger days Stan was on Liverpool FC's books as an amateur and played regularly for the Radio Merseyside team. Now in his early seventies he continues to be much in demand particularly on the club circuit and his humorous record released in 2006 for the World Cup Finals was a chart success reaching number 15 in the UK singles charts. He was also the first major comic to film a video at the Cavern Club and now has his name inscribed on a brick in Mathew Street.

Opposite: Stan at Fort Perch Rock, New Brighton. (Right)Smiling Stan talking about Germans bombing his Liverpool home.

THE ROBBINS

A family that oozes talent. Ted and Kate are just two of the great Robbins Clan.

Mike and Betty Robbins had five children all of whom have enjoyed varying degrees of success in the world of show business. The best known are Kate born 21 August 1960 and Ted four years earlier. Jane, Emma and Amy make up the family. The family home was at Mount Road, Higher Bebington. Kate attended Wirral Grammar School and from an early age was doing impressions. A teacher remarked that she would get nowhere in life doing silly voices. She went on to provide most of the female impersonations in the popular TV series Spitting Image. Among her specialities were Cilla Black, Princess Anne and Margaret Thatcher. She got her first TV break in Crossroads in 1981 . As part of the storyline, she released a single called More 'Than in Love' which reached number 2 in the UK charts. She also wrote the original well known theme tune to 'Surprise, Surprise' and has recently taken to acting in feature films.

Ted went to Liverpool University to study for a degree in English and Drama. He was also a redcoat at Butlins Holiday Camps. He is best known as a presenter of quiz shows and is regarded as one of the best warm up artists in the business, as well as being an accomplished after-dinner speaker. He now lives in Rossendale with his wife Judy and their two children Jack and Molly. He currently presents a morning show on BBC Radio Lancashire.

Emma is a successful session singer but is probably best known as one of the trio of girl singers in the TV advertisement 'Sheila's Wheels' whilst Amy played the part of Dr Jill Weatherill in Heartbeat. Kate, Emma and Jane all sang together as part of a girl band. Jane is a talented sculptress.

Their father,Mike, was a former Butlins redcoat who married Betty, Paul McCartney's cousin. Betty twelve years older than Paul, lived in Boaler Street and often looked after Paul and his younger brother Michael. In 1957 the McCartney family visited Butlins Filey Camp when Mike and Betty were both 'redcoats.' Mike encouraged Paul and Michael to enter a talent competition and they sang the Everly Brothers classic 'Bye Bye Love'. Paul also sang solo 'Long Tall Sally.' Mike and Betty later ran a pub, The Fox and Hounds in Gosbrook Road, Caversham, Berkshire which Paul and John Lennon visited in April 1960 and performed as the 'Nurk Twins.'

In 2000 Paul commissioned Jane Robbins to create a life size statue of his late wife Linda cradling a dog in her arms.

The rocking and rolling Robbins clan (opposite)

	...amos, Vincent R.	161
	...lams, Edith G.	163
	...ymons, Margaret A.	163
	Hebden, Percy	165
32	Hebden, Ivy	165
133	Williams, Georgina	167
1134	Pierce, John D.	169
1135	Pierce, Eileen	169
1136	Pierce, Mark	169
1137	**Robbins, Elizabeth W.**	171
1138	**Robbins, Edward M.**	171
1139	**Robbins, David M.**	171
1140	*5 Jul 80*—**Robbins, Jane M.**	171
1141	Jones, William	173
1142	Jones, William H.	173
1143	Hall, Annette G C.	175
1144	Hall, Graham S.	175

MOUNT ROAD

She is an accomplished actress; creatot of crime classic thrillers, TV screenwriter and a novelist- meet Lynda La Plante.

Born Lynda Titchmarsh on 15 March 1946, she attended Streatham House School in Victoria Road, Crosby at the same time as Nigel Rees author of the best selling Grafitti books and BBC Radio Four presenter. Lynda was brought up at 38 Coronation Drive in Great Crosby. The family later lived at 116 Moor Lane, Crosby. She left Merseyside at the age of sixteen to study at RADA in London having put down her age as twenty on the application form. Although acting, which included a part in Z Cars and in the cult children's comedy , Rentaghost in the sixties and also in Minder and The Sweeney in the seventies was her first passion, she had always dabbled in writing and had her first script accepted in 1983 cutting her teeth on the TV drama, Widows. She has since gone on to receive international acclaim for her work particularly with 'Prime Suspect' the popular TV series starring Helen Mirren as DCI Jane Tennison. She has written well over twenty novels and thirty plus television series . Despite not living in Liverpool she is fiercely proud of her roots and returns to the area whenever she can. On a recent visit she fondly described visiting a city centre pub at lunchtime not knowing anyone present but feeling she knew everyone by the time she left. She has received numerous awards for her writing but one of her proudest was the Liverpool Echo Arts award which she received in 1997 for the best TV writer for the series 'Trial and Retribution'. She has in the past contributed to the John Moores University by establishing a creative writing scholarship for young people to pursue a career in writing. Lynda was awarded the CBE in the 2008 Queen's Birthday Honours List. She lives in Kingston, Surrey with her son Lorcan.

Lyna La Plante with Prime Suspect star Helen Mirren (above) and on a visit to JMU in Liverpool (below). The actress turned screenwriter and novelist - liverpool's Lynda.

CORONATION DRIVE

Warwi
Mrs
ne Misses Edith D. & E
aine Rt. S
Jacobsen Miss Emily
22 Lodge Wilfred O
24 Barclay Mrs. Hilda Madeline
26 Birkett Miss Irene
28 Baker Herbt. Geo
mid- 30 Rich David
Woodvil
32 Cromie Fredk
34 Thomas Edwd. Wellington
36 Keenan Geo
38 Titchmarsh Wm
40 Corns Mrs. Winifred B
42 Lee Wltr. Jas
44 Worrall Mrs. M
46 Hermon Mrs. Beatrice
48 Riddiough Eric bank manage
50 Griffiths Danl. E
52 Whyte Patrick Hy
52AIson Miss Dorothy
52BIson Miss Ann Hare
54 Hudson Mrs. M. A
56 Marston Mrs. Edith

LYNDA LA PLANTE

RITA HUNTER

Rita Hunter was a musical mould-breaker on the international stage. She had the finest voice in England, said Milan's opera critics.

She acquired her Christian name when her parents went to see the film ' Rio Rita '. They were celebrating that, after 20 years of marriage, a baby was on the way and Rita was duly born on 15 August 1933.The family home was at 27 Limekiln Lane in Poulton, Wallasey and Rita attended Poulton Primary and Manor Road Secondary Schools. Her father Charles worked as a boilermaker at Cammell Laird's shipyard and later made his living on the ferries and was also producer for the Wallasey Grand Opera Company. Whilst at school Rita appeared with her father's company. She came up the hard way, singing in Liverpool

clubs and when she left school at 15 joined a touring pantomime company telling them she was 17. Roy Castle was also a member. She received voice training with Liverpool's leading teacher Edwin Francis who was based at Byrom's Studios, 27 Houghton Street, Liverpool 1. It was here that she met and formed a life-long friendship with fellow pupil Alberto Remedios. In 1953 her road to fame began when she secured a position with the Italian Opera Company based in Milan and she was acclaimed to have the finest voice in England. By 1957 she was singing with the Carl Rosa Opera Company appearing with them at the Royal Court Theatre in May of that year, alongside Valerie Griffiths, another Merseysider who was brought up at 19 Tudor Avenue, Bebington. In 1980 Rita was honoured with the OBE, but by now her appearances in Britain were becoming less frequent although she toured Britain in 1986 when she appeared on 'Wogan' and returned to Liverpool one last time in 1992 when she sang at the Royal Gala Concert attended by the Spanish King and Queen to celebrate the return of the tall ships. She was, however, still in great demand in Australia where she had moved in 1981. She died in Sydney on 29 April 2001. At her funeral she was described as a 'lovely person, great fun to be around and strong in her beliefs which reflected her earthy Liverpool background.' She said in the first line of her autobiography, which was published in 1986. that she was 'proud of her Merseyside heritage.' She will be remembered as one of the great Wagnerian sopranos of the late 20th century.

Rita, a voice a in a million in Italy (opposite); A young Ms Hunter in Liverpool (above).

DAVID YIP

David Yip, writer and actor, is a local talent who made a dramatic impact in Brookside and films. He also appeared in the BBC's Liverpool Nativity screened on BBC 2008.

The family home from 1948 was at 5 Duke Terrace which was situated on the edge of the city's famous Chinese quarter, tucked away behind Duke Street.

An accomplished actor best known for his role as Johnny Ho in the 1981 BBC drama series ' The Chinese Detective', David was born on 4 June 1951 one of ten children to a Chinese seaman and a white Liverpool mother.

David's childhood memories are of a home that was almost fenced-off due to new properties being built all around them, and that the postmen used to have difficulty locating it.

There were just nine houses in the terrace and David and his younger brother Stephen can still recall the names of the other residents.He also looks back in amazement on how twelve people managed to live in a house with just six rooms. In 1966 the family moved to 7 Bold Place off Berry Street where they lived until the mid-eighties.

David and his siblings attended Pleasant Street School close to Mount Pleasant, and from the age of eleven he was a pupil at Toxteth Technical College in Aigburth Road. On leaving school he worked for a while as a clerk for British Rail in Edge Hill. In his lunch break he would read Samuel Beckett's 'Waiting for Godot' and it was this more than anything that inspired him to become a writer and actor.

He landed a job as assistant stage manager at the Neptune Theatre in Hanover Street and later joined the Everyman before training as an actor with Joan Littlewood's company in London. He has lived in London ever since but visits Liverpool on a regular basis to see his family and friends.

He is a great champion of Liverpool and is constantly astounded at the amount of talent it produces, and has said that

once people achieve success in Liverpool they seem to retain their vitality, and do not just sit back, be they politicians, actors, doctors or footballers. He also remembers his childhood with affection stating: " The kids I played with were all colours and it never crossed my mind that we were not anything else than English or British – or simply Scousers."

His brother Stephen runs the famous charity KIND – Kids in Need and Distress.

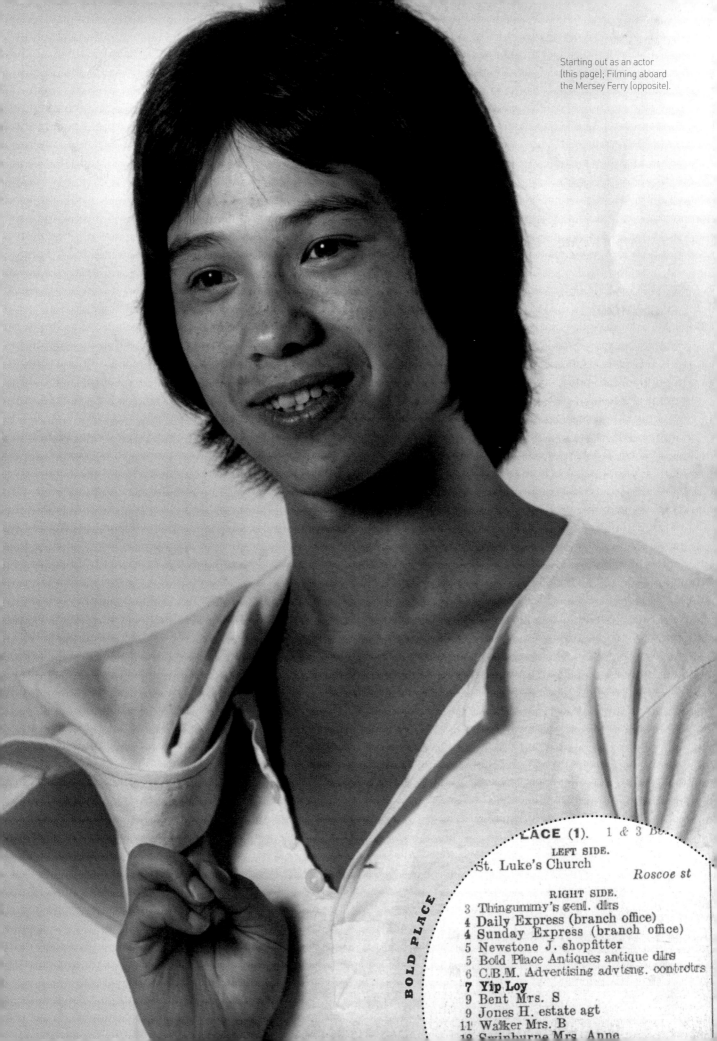

Starting out as an actor (this page); Filming aboard the Mersey Ferry (opposite).

BOLD PLACE

PLACE (1).   1 & 3 BO...

LEFT SIDE.
St. Luke's Church   Roscoe st

RIGHT SIDE.
3 Thingummy's genl. dlrs
4 **Daily Express** (branch office)
4 Sunday Express (branch office)
5 Newstone J. shopfitter
5 Bold Place Antiques antique dlrs
6 C.B.M. Advertising advtsng. contrctrs
7 **Yip Loy**
9 Bent Mrs. S
9 Jones H. estate agt
11 Walker Mrs. B
12 Swinburne Mrs. Anne

ELVIS COSTELLO

Declan McManus, alias Elvis
Costello, one of the most respected musicians in the
world (above) and in pensive
mood (opposite).

Elvis Costello became a life-long Beatles fan when, on a visit to Birkenhead in 1963, a girl gave him a publicity photograph of the band. He became one of the most respected and versatile rock musicians in the world eventually working playimng and co-writing with Paul McCartney.

Born Declan Patrick McManus on 25 August 1954 in London, he was christened in Birkenhead. Declan's grandfather Patrick McManus was also a musician and lived in Cathcart Street, Birkenhead.

His mother Mary was born in Liverpool and his father Ronald but known as Ross, in Conway Street, Birkenhead. Ross McManus born in 1927 was a well-known bandleader and balladeer who appeared regularly on BBC Radio's Light Programme 'Parade of the Pops' and recorded a version of the Beatles 'The Long and Winding Road'.

In 1961 he tied with Billy Fury in the 'Melody Maker' best singer poll.

The young Declan became a life-long Beatles fan when, on a visit to Birkenhead in 1963, a girl gave him a publicity photograph of the band. He has since written songs with Paul McCartney.

He went to school in London but his final two years schooling were at St Francis Xavier Grammar School in Shaw Street, Liverpool.

His parents split up when he was fifteen and he went to live with his mother in Oxton.

His mother had worked for a while in NEMS record store in Whitechapel.

She was also, in the late forties, an unpaid usher at the Philharmonic Hall.

He had relatives in Belmont Road, Anfield, and was a regular visitor to their home.

On Merseyside he played in a four-piece band as a solo singer and venues included the Yankee Clipper, The Temple Bar in Liverpool and the British Legion in Birkenhead. His first ever TV performance was filmed at Eric's in Mathew Street.

He worked briefly as a computer operator at the Midland Bank Computer Centre in Bootle but changed his name to Elvis Costello in 1977.

Costello is his mother's maiden name.

Several of his songs have a Mersey connection including 'The Angels Wanna Wear My Red Shoes 'which was written when he was on a train travelling between Runcorn and Lime Street.

'Veronica' and 'Last Boat Leaving' are set in Birkenhead specifically in his grandmother's home with its view of the river. His most successful recording was 'Oliver's Army' which reached number 2 in the UK single charts. Apart from the Beatles, one passion is Liverpool Football club. He has followed them since visiting Anfield for the first time in the mid sixties. He married the jazz singer Dianne Krall on 11 December 2003 and the couple live in New York City with their twin sons Dexter and Frank, who were born in December 2006. In June 2008 he performed at the Philharmonic Hall with the Royal Philharmonic Orchestra.

Teresa
Beckwith st
John shipwright
uston Jas. Eric joiner
Connell Wm. secondhand booksllr
edmond Eugene baker
Towers Chas. labourer
Kelly Chas. tailors' presser
4 Moiseff Stephen labourer
126 Johnson Mrs. Bertha
128 Earl Jn. labourer
130 Croxon Mrs. Gertrude
132 Greenwood Miss Annie
134 McManus Patrick musician
136 Woolley Miss Florence Mabel
138 George Thomas labourer
140 McArdle Thos. carter
142 Sloan Michl. labourer
144 Murphy Hy

CATHCART STREET

CARLA LANE

Carla Lane, poet, author, TV writer with hits such as Liver Birds, Butterflies and Bread. She is one of the small screen's most successful female writers. But for this vegetarian, animal welfare remains her ultimate driving passion.

Born Ramona Barrack in 1937 when her mother Ivy was just eighteen years of age and her father nineteen. Her father was a ships engineer and spent a lot of time away from home and died aged just fifty one. The family home was in Eaton Road, West Derby.

Convent-educated Carla, with her brother Ramon and sister Marna, spent a lot of time at their maternal grandparents Forans home in the Wirral.

Her paternal grandparents lived at 6 Colwyn Street, Old Swan and her grandfather John was the the Chief Inspector of the R.S.P.C.A which no doubt influenced the young Ramona's love of animals.

A lot of her leisure time was spent at the Silver Blades Ice Rink in Prescot Road were she met her future husband Eric Hollins.

It was a whirlwind romance and she married at the age of seventeen.

The couple divorced and had two sons: Carl, born in 1954, and Nigel in 1956. Their first home was a tiny bedsit in Wallasey before they went to live with Eric's parents, who were the licensees of The Blue Ball Hotel at 105 Prescot Street Low Hill before moving to a flat in Aigburth. Ramona worked on the cosmetic counter at the Bon Marche Fashion Store in Church Street and then for a short while on an assembly line at the Automatic in Edge Lane putting telephone dials together.

She had joined the Liverpool Writers' Club which was based above the Rembrandt Club at 12 Slater Street. It was from these humble beginnings and now known as Carla Lane that she developed her talent for writing which culminated in the popular TV series 'The Liverbirds' first screened in 1970. This was followed by the equally successful' Bread' which was set in the Dingle, and 'Butterflies'. With her success she was able to purchase 'Claremont' an imposing mansion in Sandfield Park, West Derby, which she shared with her family including her mother and an assortment of animals.

As a young child she had often walked past Claremont and dreamt of living there one day. The house is now a luxury apartment block.

Carla now lives in the South of England and is an active campaigner on behalf of animals. She was a great friend of the late Linda McCartney through their love of animals and wrote two songs for Linda's Wild Prairie album. Paul McCartney and Linda also appeared in an episode of Bread which was screened in October 1988.

Carla is never happier than when she is with her beloved animals (opposite); Carla in happy-go-lucky mode (above).

insur. agt
rs. Emma
Mrs. Madge

Alvanley rd

...te Mrs. Ada Eliz
...eece Harold
Leak Sam timber agt
footpath to Leyfield rd
289 Jones Hugo Franklin assistant insur. supt
291 Burroughs Albt. W
293 Martin Miss Margt
Danescourt rd
299 Lunt Sydney H
301 Rutter Miss H. Rose
303 Ashbury Geo. Thos
305 Osbourn Fredk
307 Haddock Arth
309 Barrack Gordon engnr
Kingscourt rd

EATON ROAD

MATHEW STREET

Once a street of warehouses-Apples (how ironic). It later became the focal point of music with The Cavern and Eric's. Now it's the Cavern Quarter.

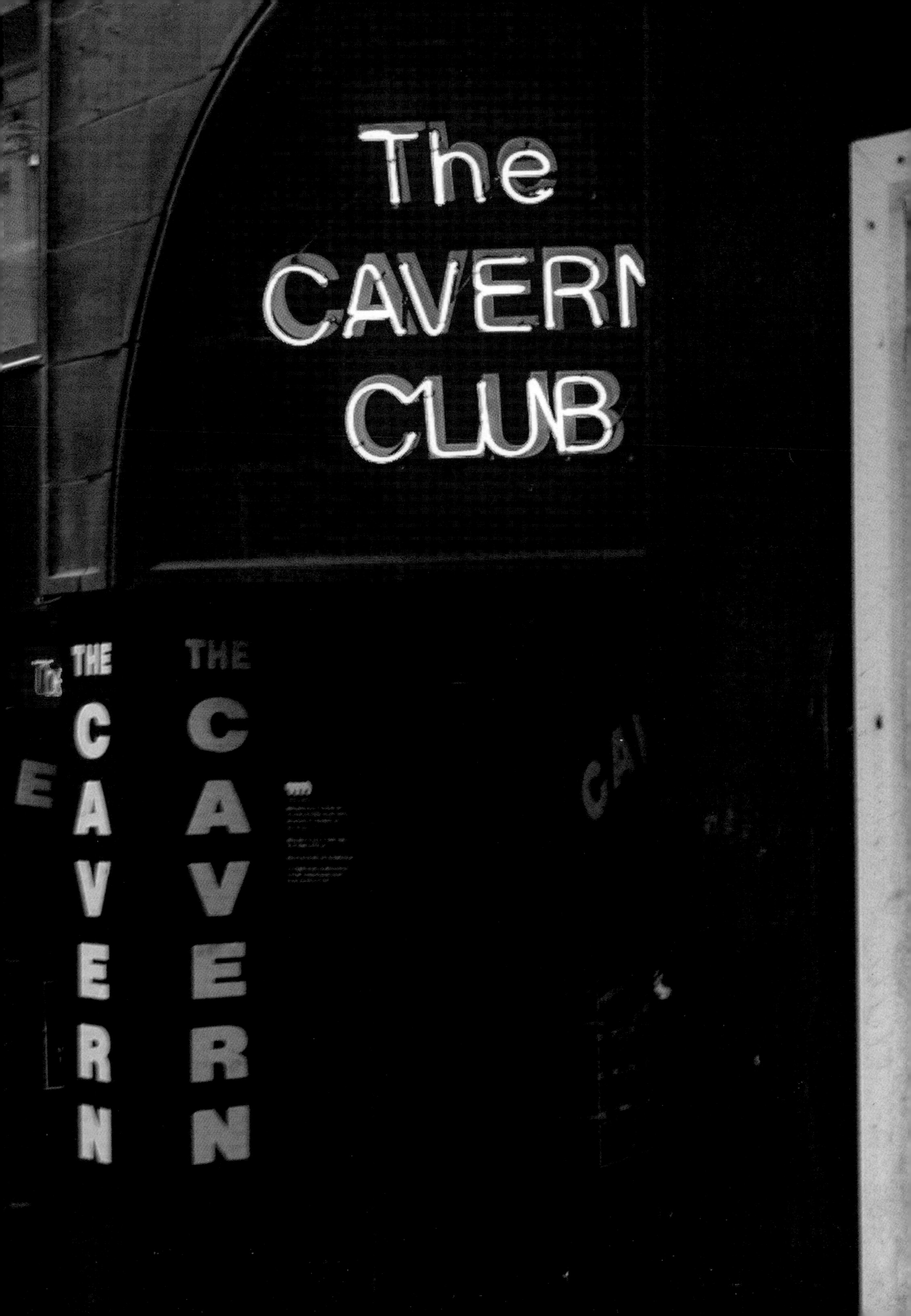
The
CLUB
THE
CAVERN
THE
CAVERN

PATRICIA ROUTLEDGE

Star of stage and screen, Patricia Routledge is a winner of many Scouseology personality awards - the nation's favourite funny woman.

Known to millions of TV viewers as Hyacinth Bucket (pronounced Bouquet), Pat was born on 17 February 1929. The family lived at 2 Whitfield Street in Tranmere, Birkenhead. Her father Isaac ran a gent's outfitters at 36 Church Road close to the family home. Her mother was Catherine. During the war when Birkenhead was heavily bombed her father built a reinforced bunker in his shop and the family slept there for weeks on end. Pat and her brother Graham would play board games there and do their homework. At the end of the war the family went to live at 48 Heyville Road, Higher Bebington. She was educated firstly at Mersey Park Primary School in Elm Road and took part in several school plays. At the age of eleven she went to Birkenhead High School for Girls in Devonshire Place, Claughton where she took elocution and singing lessons and was encouraged in her desire to become an actress by her English teacher. She went on to read English at Liverpool University while keeping up her interest in acting. She graduated in English Literature and Language in 1951 and was to train as a teacher, but this plan was changed after she successfully auditioned at the Liverpool Playhouse. She made her stage debut in Shakespeare at the Playhouse in August 1952. After moving to London her career took off and she has never been short of offers of work in theatre and television. Her talents have given her many parts in serious acting to the more light hearted parts such as the nationally loved Hyacinth Bucket! Her husband in 'Keeping Up Appearances ' was played by Clive Swift another Merseysider. The series ended at her request in 1995. In 1996 she played the lead role in Hetty Wainwright Investigates another long running series. In 1993 at a service at Liverpool's Anglican Cathedral she was granted an honorary degree by John Moores University and also that year was awarded the OBE. In 1999 she was presented with an honorary degree at her old university. She was made a commander of the British Empire in 2004. Now living in the South of England she still retains her contact with Merseyside which has included a spell as president of Claire House.

Patricia early in her sparkling career (opposite);
Young Ms Routledge in Liverpool and as hilarious dragon Hyacinth Bouquet (above).

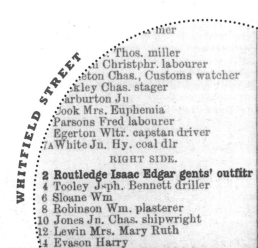

163

NICHOLAS MONSARRAT

The author wrote one of the best maritime novels of the 20th century The Crule Sea and his literary career set sail from Liverpool

Nicholas John Turney Monsarrat was born on 22 March 1910 at 11 Rodney Street, Liverpool 1. His father Keith Waldegrave Monsarrat was a distinguished surgeon, whilst his mother Marguerite was the daughter of a prosperous tradesman in the city. Nicholas spent five miserable years at Winchester school before studying law at Trinity College, Cambridge graduating in 1931. On his return to Liverpool he worked as a solicitor for a short period before deciding to leave Liverpool for London. Utterly bored with law he had commenced writing as a hobby and he departed for London with a half finished manuscript under his arm and £40 in his pocket. On arriving in London he was astounded at the level of poverty he encountered and he became an advocate of better living conditions for the capital's poor. His first three novels published between 1934 and 1937 and now out of print were realistic treatments of the social problems he encountered. As a child he had been fascinated with the River Mersey and spent many hours at the Pier Head particularly in the winter months observing the high tides and fantasising about a life at sea. It was this and his distinguished service in the Royal Navy during and after World War 2 that influenced his classic ' The Cruel Sea ' published in 1951 and widely acclaimed as one of the best novels of the 20th century, and which was later made into a film starring Jack Hawkins. He was responsible for numerous other classics including 'The Tribe that Lost Its Head' and 'The Story of Esther Costello'. His final work 'The Master Mariner' unfinished at the time of his death but published in incomplete form. The sea was a source of fascination to him throughout his life and he spent his latter years living in Guernsey and then Gozo, Maltas smaller sister island. He had said that he had been born near the sea in Liverpool and when he died wished to be laid at rest at sea. He died on the 8 August 1979 and in accordance with his wishes he was buried off the English coast. There is a plaque on the wall of 11 Rodney Street dedicated to him.

Writer reflecting on his life in Rodney Street (below); Opposite the Grand Mariner of literature (opposite).

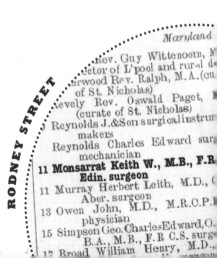

TONY BOOTH

Tony Booth became famous as the 'Scouse Git' in Till Death Us Do Part, but there was much more to this actor than appearing in a famous BBC sitcom – just ask the in-laws.

FERNDALE ROAD

..cKenna Jas
..Burns Mrs. E
3 Grubb Chas
5 Molloy Mrs. Mar
7 Jones Mrs. A. M
9 Hughes Hugh
11 Millhouse Mrs. L
13 Lyners Albt
15 **Booth Geo. Hy**
17 Skeldon Jn
19 Chadwick Miss C
21 Kerrigan Mrs. I
23 Walpole Thos. F
25 Jones Mrs. M
27 Rhoden Miss An
29 Harrison Chas
31 Jackson Chas

These days though he is probably better known as ex Prime Minister Tony Blair's father-in-law and father of Cherie, he made his name in the 1960's TV sit-com " Till Death Us Do Part ". He played the role of " The Scouse git ", Alf Garnett's son-in-law Mike Rawlins. Born 9 October 1931 to Vera and George the family home was at 15 Ferndale Road, Waterloo a three bedroomed terraced house which was shared with Tonys grandparents, Robert and Matilda Thompson. His father spent a lot of time at sea and Tony was much influenced by his grandfather in his early years. His paternal grandparents Sidney and Virginia Booth lived close by at 16 Sunnyside Road, a semi-detached house which looked out onto open fields and was considered quite posh. In 1937 he contracted diphtheria and spent some time in a special unit at Fazakerly Hospital. Tony was educated, firstly at St Edmunds Primary School in Oxford Road, Waterloo and from 1943 at St Mary's College in Crosby run by the Christian Brothers which he hated. Ironically his family were devout Catholics and hoped that Tony would enter the Priesthood and he served as an   altar boy at St Edmunds Church from the ages of six until he was eighteen. He attended Latin lessons at Park House in Crosby a women's nursing home run by nuns. His daughter Cherie was educated at Seafield Convent School in Crosby. Cherie and her younger sister Lyndsey are the daughters of Gale, Tonys first wife. He married Pat Phoenix the Coronation Street actress one week before her death in 1986 in hospital in Cheadle, after the couple had lived together for a number of years. On leaving school he first worked at the American Consulate in the Cunard Building at the Pierhead, in the immigration section. There then followed a period of National Service and on discharge he secured employment as an accounts clerk with the Cunard Line. Whilst undoubtedly his private life has been colourful including four marriages and eight children and much hell raising , he is a talented versatile actor in both the comedy field, and in more recent times in a number of serious roles. He is still acting and remains an active supporter of the Labour Party. After a period living in Ireland he currently lives in Todmorden in West Yorkshire.

Tony Booth well versed in straight and comedy drama. He is also father to Cherie Booth and Tony's father -in-law too..

GEOFFREY HUGHES

Geoffrey Hughes made his name as a star in many TV series including Eddie Yates in Coronation Street. He went on to appear in Heartbeat and The Royle Family and he is proud to be a patron of the Unity Theatre in Liverpool.

Geoffrey Hughes: TV star with top shows on his CV (above);
A Rover returns: Eddie Yates in Coronation Street (opposite).

Geoffrey was born on 2 February 1944 in Wallasey moving to Norris Green at the age of six.

He attended Abbotsford Road Senior School (see below) and it was a teacher there who gave him his first taste for the stage.

With his teacher's encouragement he joined the Unity Theatre where he did several jobs including painting scenery before being given small parts.

He was also a member of the 29th Liverpool Company of the Boys Brigade.

His childhood memories of Liverpool include him climbing over the wall of Lord Sefton's estate to steal conkers .

He developed his sense of humour by observing his father who worked for a while on the docks and also at Capenhurst.

Geoffrey studied at Newcastle University and commenced his career in repertory at the Victoria Theatre in Stoke - On-Trent.

Apart from Eddie Yates in Coronation Street, he is well known as Twiggy in the 'Royle Family', Onslow in 'Keeping up Appearances' and Vernon in 'Heartbeat.'

He was also the voice of Paul McCartney in the Beatles animated film Yellow Submarine. In December 2007 he played the part of the Angel Gabriel in the BBC TV production Liverpool Nativity – the largest ever TV production staged on Liverpool's streets with a technical crew of 150.

The cast numbered 300 which as well as Geoffrey included fellow Liverpudlians Paul Barber, Jennifer Ellison, Louis Emerick, Joe Mc Gann, Cathy Tyson and David Yip.

Rhyl born Nerys Hughes of Liver Birds fame also appeared. The production was written by Liverpool-born Mark Davies Markham.

A keen sailor, who first sailed in Liverpool when he was seventeen, Geoffrey now lives on the Isle of Wight with his wife Sue.

In recent years he has overcome prostate cancer and was part of a campaign to get men to see their GPs more.

Despite not playing the part for 25 years, Geoffrey is probably best-remembered as Hilda Ogden's lodger, Eddie Yeats in Coronation Street.

MICHAEL HOLLIDAY

Michael was a singer once called England's Bing Crosby.
Sadly, his life ended far too early.
His song 'Starry Eyed' is a true classic.

He was born Norman Alexander Milne on 25 November 1924. His father Robert was a seafarer who originated from New Zealand whilst his mother Cissie was of Irish origin He had two brothers Robert and David. The family home was at 40 St Agnes Road in Kirkdale.He attended St Alphonsus School in Back Great Mersey Street and then had a series of jobs including delivering milk, working at a butchers in St Johns Market and at Silvermere dry cleaners in Moorfields. He then followed in his father's footsteps and joined the Merchant Navy before transferring to the Royal Navy with whom he saw active service towards the end of the Second World War. On leave in Liverpool he met his future wife Marjorie Lloyd who lived in Harlow Street, Toxteth. They were married at Brougham Terrace Registry Office, West Derby Road. On his discharge from the Navy he sang in local pubs and with the help of his brother Robert, who ran the catering side at Butlins, obtained bookings at various holiday camps including Pwlhelli in North Wales. He also performed regularly at the Burtonwood Airforce base near Warrington. He was now performing as Michael Holliday. In 1953 and just as he was about to record his first song 'The Yellow Rose Of Texas', which did not chart his brother Robert died, a tragedy that would affect Michael for the rest of his life. He went on to have seven top twenty hits including two number ones ' The Story of My Life ' in 1958 and ' Starry Eyed ' in 1960. On stage he appeared confident and relaxed but he was, in fact, a born worrier and beset by financial problems. On 29 October 1963 he committed suicide in Croydon, Surrey by way of a suspected drugs overdose leaving a note for his wife which read ' by the time you read this I will be in the land of nod '. He was cremated at Anfield Crematorium. An overdose of tablets tragically cut short his career at the relatively young age of 38. His rich singing voice, which is still popular today, has been likened to that of Bing Crosby and also Perry Como. His premature death cut short a career which had been enjoyed by millions.

His songs are still played on the airwaves .

The man next door , Michaele Holliday
- tragic hit maker (opposite).

ST AGNES ROAD

.Jt. Leslie
Mrs. Mary
ur Michl
illiams Mrs
Jatt Rd
Scully Thos
26 McGlone Thos
28 McEwan Leonard Alex
30 Kelly Jsph
32 Heaton Thos
34 Palen Jn
36 Dempsey Arth
38 McLeod Miss Mary Ellen
40 Milne Rt. labourer
42 Deane Danl
44 Heyes Jsph. labourer
46 Ebbutt Mrs. E

Fonthill rd .

ST. AIDAN'S TER. CLAUGHTON.
Shrewsbury road North.
LEFT SIDE.

LEONARD ROSSITER

Leonard Rossiter was an actor for all seasons. A true perfectionist - he didn't suffer fools gladly on and off stage .

Leonard was born on 21 October 1926 in Cretan Road, Wavertree above his father's barbers shop the family later moving to 65 Montrovia Crescent, Fazakerley. The youngest of two children to John and Elizabeth Rossiter, his elder brother was also called John. His father was a volunteer ambulance driver during the war and was killed whilst on duty taking the injured to hospital. Leonard was educated firstly at Granby Street County Primary School and then the Liverpool Collegiate Grammar School in Shaw Street where he was vice captain, although apparently not the most popular with other pupils. He excelled at languages and was also an excellent sportsman captaining both the football and cricket teams. He was also a member of the school drama society. He was conscripted towards the end of the war and spent some time in Germany in the Education Corps attaining the rank of Sergeant. Demobbed in 1947 he worked as a clerk for seven years in the claims department at the Commercial Union Assurance Company Ltd in Derby House, Exchange Buildings in Tithebarn Street. One of his colleagues was the late Michael Williams who became an actor and was married to Dame Judy Dench. Leonard's own acting ability was apparent by his performances as an amateur with the Wavertree Community Centre Players who had premises in Penny Lane and the Adastra group in Speke. He turned professional at the age of 27 in 1954 and in 1961 he played the part of Inspector Bamber in' Z Cars' the TV series based in Kirkby new town. He is, however, best remembered for his role in the 1976 series ' The Rise and Fall of Reginald Perrin ' and his brilliant portrayal of Rigsby in ' Rising Damp '. He also spilled Cinzano over Joan Colilns in one of TV best known commercials. Leonard was a shy man who led a very private life and hated publicity. He died on 5 October 1984 as he sat in the dressing room whilst waiting to go on stage in a performance of Joe Orton's play ' Loot '. His comparatively early death was a great shock as he kept himself fit playing squash and tennis regularly and he had been given the 'all clear' by his doctor before accepting his role in Loot.

He left behind his second wife Gillian and daughter Camilla.

Leonard as Rigsby in Rising Damp (opposite); and (above) relaxing with mum Elizabeth Rossiter.

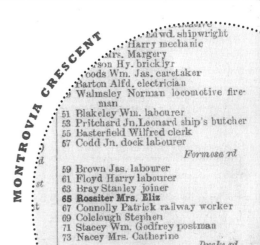

MONTROVIA CRESCENT

Edwd. shipwright
Harry mechanic
Mrs. Margery
son Hy. bricklyr
oods Wm. Jas. caretaker
Barton Alfd. electrician
Walmsley Norman locomotive fireman
51 Blakeley Wm. labourer
53 Pritchard Jn.Leonard ship's butcher
55 Basterfield Wilfred clerk
57 Codd Jn. dock labourer
Formosa rd

59 Brown Jas. labourer
61 Floyd Harry labourer
63 Bray Stanley joiner
65 Rossiter Mrs. Eliz
67 Connolly Patrick railway worker
69 Colclough Stephen
71 Stacey Wm. Godfrey postman
73 Nacey Mrs. Catherine
Drake rd
RIGHT SIDE.

SCOTLAND ROAD

Scotland Road ... Scottie Road, it's a place all Scousers know. The nation knows it. It's changed just like the city itself.

CHURCH STREET

ALAN DURBAND

The former teacher who taught Paul McCartney. Alan Durband sitting in the auditiorium at the Everyman Theatre.

Alan 'Dusty' Durband was a teacher who became a theatrical visionary who helped establish Liverpool as a centre of creative excellence. His legacy lives on.

Alan was born in 1927 in Drysdale Street, Liverpool 8 an only child to Joseph and Edith Durband. His father was a ship's carpenter who spent a lot of time away at sea and Alan was brought up mainly by his mother. He attended Mathew Arnold Primary School in Dingle Lane and at the age of eleven passed the scholarship to the Liverpool Institute in Mount Street, where he became, for a brief period, head boy. The family moved to 12 Esher Road, Kensington while Alan was at the Institute. An outstanding scholar he graduated to Cambridge University but not before he had completed his National Service. A lifelong pacifist he refused to join the Armed forces and spent 18 months as a 'Bevan boy' working in the mines. It was here that he earned the nickname 'Dusty' which would remain with him for the rest of his life. Following graduation from Cambridge he became a teacher at his old school Liverpool Institute where he taught English. He was always referred to by the pupils as 'Dusty Durband.' One of his students was Paul McCartney who described Dusty as his favourite teacher. He was extremely popular with the boys particularly his series of text books, English Workshop, which he had written in 1959 and which were used by many schools in the UK.

Now married he lived wih his wife and family at 24 Hillside Road in Woolton. In 1962 he joined the staff at C F Mott Teachers Training College in Huyton attaining the position of head of English. His interest in the arts had developed whilst at Cambridge and he produced several dramas and plays. He was a motivating force behind the creation of the Everyman Theatre in Hope Street which had opened in 1964 and gave opportunities to new playwrights including a young Willy Russell. Alan would serve the Everyman for more thanr 20 years in several leading capacities and helped raise thousands of pounds. In his latter years he spent a lot of time in Finestrat, Spain, where he died in September 1994 aged 67. His memory is served by a commemorative plaque at the Everyman, and his old brief case is cast in stone close to the Institute at the top of Mount Street. The Institute, now LIPA, has named his old classroom 32 the Alan Durband room. Willy Russell described him as an 'extraordinary man' while Brian Jacques, who became a successful children's author, would comment "but for Alan I would not be here."

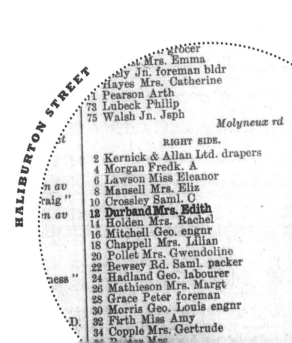

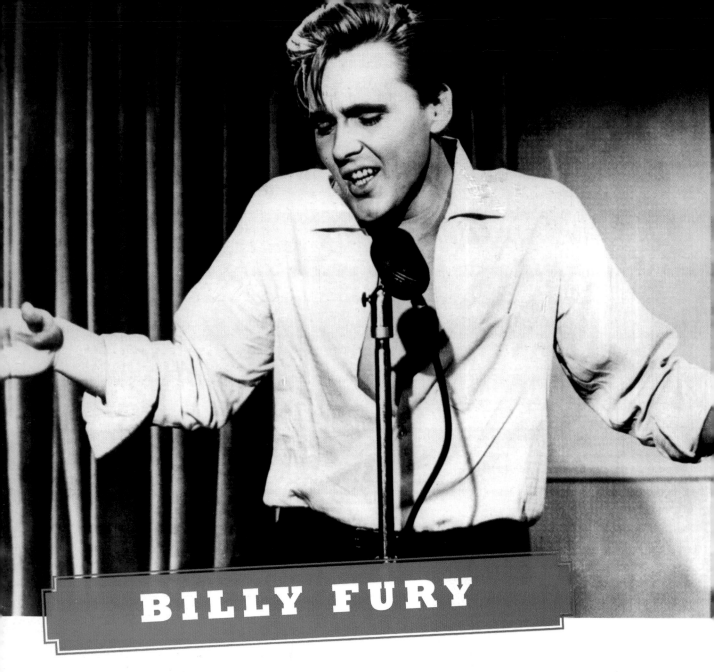

BILLY FURY

Billy Fury was Liverpool's answer to Elvis. He enjoyed a massive following in the UK with 19 top twenty hits and the much-loved star, who died tragically early, is immortalised with a statue in his home town.

Ronald Wycherly was born on 17 April 1940 at Smithdown Road General Hospital to Sarah Jane Homer (known as Jean) and Albert Edward Wycherly. They had met whilst working at the same shoe repairers. They married in 1939 and lived at 2 Sefton Square off High Park, Liverpool 8. Their second child Albert was born on 26 June 1943.

The Wycherlys then moved to 34 Haliburton Street off Park Road.

Albert senior was a shoe 'mechanic' who had his own shop on Park Road. Ronnie, as he was known to his family and friends, attended St Silas's Primary school at the same time as Ringo Starr, and also Billy

HALIBURTON STREET

....annah
...bt. Edwd
... Jn. Jas
...s Mrs. Sarah Ann
...ions Alex
...dwards Mrs. Catherine
...Charnock Thos. crane driver
... Arnold Mrs. Martha

Digby

24 Fearnyough Jsph
26 Poole Chas. Hy. cooper
28 Masters Chas. mariner
30 Bullock Rd
32 Wignall Mrs. Margt
34 Wycherley Albt
36 Weisske Jn. Wm
38 Crosbie Albt. Edwd. motor driv
40 Winks Chas. Harvey
42 Crane Wm. Jn
44 Huxley Wm
46 Copeland Mrs. Kathln
48 Williams Wm Jn boot repr

Hatton who would later become a member of the Fourmost and who was a good friend of Ronnies.

At the age of six Ronnie contracted rheumatic fever and was admitted to Alder Hey Childrens Hospital causing him to miss a lot of schooling.

AT the age of eleven he was transferred to Wellington Road Secondary Modern in the Dingle but his education continued to suffer due to continuing poor health. Consequently he left school at 15 with no formal qualifications.

However from an early age he had developed a talent for music and in 1954 his parents bought him a guitar at Frank Hessys in Stanley Street.

His first job at Ellisons Engineering Works was spent mainly making tea for the welders but poor behaviour resulted in his dismissal. He then worked for the Alexandra Towing Company who had offices in Park Road near his home, as a deckhand before again being sacked. Ronnie later worked briefly for Joshua Harris, Wholesalers in London Road before being dismissed yet again.

If his employment record was poor he was by now establishing himself as a singer and this brought him to the attention of the pop impresario Larry Parnes who quickly signed him up following an appearance at the Essoldo Cinema in Birkenhead and changed his name to Billy Fury a quite ironic name as in reality he was rather shy and withdrawn. He enjoyed massive chart success in the UK which included 19 top twenty hits. Apart from visits to his family, who now lived at 87 South Mossley Hill Road he virtually severed all links with Liverpool although he always retained a strong affection for the city.

Dogged by ill health throughout his life he died on 17 January 1983 at his home in St John's Wood, London at the age of 42.

He was in the process of recording a new album and had just had a single in the charts. A memorial service was held for him at Liverpool Cathedral and his memory is honoured by an inscription on one of the Anglican Cathedral's lecturns.

There is also a bronze statue of him at the Pierhead.

In typical hip-swinging form (opposite); Billy on TV (above top); In concert (below).

BRIAN JACQUES

Brian Jacques, playwright, stand-up, poet, broadcaster and writer. One of the most successful childrens' authors in the world thanks to his Redwall books.

Brian Jacques (pronounced Jakes) was born to James and Ellen Jacques in Liverpool on 15 June 1939. He was the second eldest of three boys having an older brother Tony and a younger brother James. The family home was in Hornby Road, Bootle.

His father although of limited education encouraged his children to read books from an early age.

Brian has described him as a 'stern man' and one you did not argue with.

Educated at St John's school off Fountains Road in Kirkdale, Brian was introduced to poetry by his favourite teacher Mr Austin Thomas whom he said 'resembled Lee Marvin.'

He left school at 15 and joined the Merchant Navy and travelled the world. On his return to Liverpool he had several jobs including that of stevedore, truck driver and bus driver. For a short period he was a police constable and had the number 216D.

He was also a professional folk singer in a group with his two brothers calling themselves the Liverpool Fishermen.

It was whilst working as a truck driver and delivering milk to the Wavertree School for the Blind in Church Road North that he formed an affinity with the pupils, and began to spend his spare time there. He would write short stories for the school and his friend Alan Durband was so impressed with them that he recommended Brian to his own publisher and the famous Redwall series of books was born. He was then in his forties.

Brian based part of the books on his childhood memories of Stanley Park, its red sandstone wall reminding him of an Abbey. They have now sold millions world wide and have been published in 28 languages.

He is still a regular visitor to the park when taking his west highland terrier Terry for a walk. For a number of years he had his own programme on Radio Merseyside ' Jakestown '. His knowledge of classical music is encycloapedic.

He still lives in Liverpool and has two sons David and Marc. David is a professor of Art and has been commissioned to paint at various Children's Hospitals and Soccer Stadiums.

Brian Jacques – is there anything this Scouser can't do? (opposite) with a Redwall character and as a BBC DJ (above)

GLENDA JACKSON

Glenda has, in effect, had two careers. Firstly as an internationally-acclaimed actress and then as a politician.

Glenda May Jackson was born at 161 Market Street in Birkenhead on 9 May 1936.

Her parents, Harry and Jane, were lodging at the home of Glenda's maternal grandmother Mrs Pearce.

They soon moved to their own home a terraced house at 3 Evans Road, Hoylake but were shortly on the move again this time to nearby 21 Lake Place.

Glenda's father was known as Mick and worked as a bricklayer.

He had served in the Navy during the war, whilst her mother did part-time cleaning and barmaid jobs. The eldest of four girls, Glenda attended Hoylake Church of England Primary School firstly the infants in School Lane, and then the juniors in Market Street.

The next move was to West Kirby County Grammar School for girls which was an unhappy experience for her leaving in 1952 with just two 'O' Levels.

From Birkenhead to Hollywood (opposite); Above with Walter Mattheau; (Middle) with honorary degree and above (bottom) as a labour politcian.

She worked for brief periods at Boots the Chemists at 38 Market Street and also at Woolworths Store at 100 Market Street in Hoylake.

Glenda joined the YMCA players and appeared at the YMCA in Hoyle Road, Hoylake in pantomime, a venue the Beatles were to appear at some years later. Other stars with Hoylake connections include Daniel Craig of James Bond fame and Andy McCluskey of eighties band Orchestral Manoeuvres In The Dark. Cynthia Lennon also lived in the town.

Glenda's acting career took off when she joined the Royal Shakespeare Company in 1964 and it went into over drive when she won an Oscar for her role in Ken Russell's film 'Women In Love'.

Liverpool University bestowed an honorary doctorate in 1978 and the then Liverpool Polytechnic gave her a honorary fellowship shortly afterwards. In 1983 she opened the theatre named after her in Borough Road , Birkenhead, which was sadly demolished and replaced with flats in 2006.

She married Roy Hodges an actor and designer in 1958 and the couple had one son.They were divorced in 1978. Glenda has in effect had two careers firstly as an internationally-acclaimed actress and then as a politician.

A Labour supporter from an early age she has been Member of Parliament since 1992 for Hampstead and Highgate. In 2000 she was the unsuccessful candidate for Mayor of London. Following the 1997 general election she was made a junior minister in the first Blair goverment.

Now in her seventies it is uncertain if she will stand again at the next election.

```
                                    E.
              raham labourer                    4
           . E                                  6
         Mrs. Catherine                         8
                          Evans rd             10
    gh Mrs. Mary Ellen                         12
    all Fredk                                  14
    Aldred Jn. Bethell plumber                 16
     Gregory Harold                            18
    5 Feakes Bertie Wltr. plasterer            20
   17 Wharton Cyril T. labourer                22
   19 Norman Wm. Harold                        24
   21 Jackson Harry
   23 Dufley Alex
   25 Harris Miss                              LA
   27 Dufley Fredk. Albt
   29 Bevan Mrs. Frances A
                          Valentia rd
       Cooper Lenard motor engnr. and         113
           garage
                          Grove pl             62
```

BILLY J KRAMER

Billy J. Kramer singer-songwriter and Merseybeat idol who is still touring at home and abroad. The J in his name doesn't actually stand for anything it was John Lennon's idea.

Born William Ashton on 19 August 1943, the youngest of seven children, the family lived at 27 Hankey Drive, Bootle.

He was educated at Orrell Primary School in Aughton Road and then St George of England Secondary Modern, Fernhill Road . After leaving school Billy had various jobs including as a diesel fitter for British Rail and as a shoe salesman.

He impressed his employers at British Rail and was offered promotion and a transfer to Crewe but by now his singing career as Billy Kramer was taking off and he declined the offer.

He was playing with his group the Coasters at various clubs in Liverpool including the Cavern and appeared in Hamburg in 1960 at

HANKEY DRIVE

... ...rer
... ...ertrude
... ... Daisy
...ne Michl. dock labourer
...rke Peter Thos. labourer
...Mellor Ernest fitters' labourer
...5 Roberts Jsph. Hy. labourer
17 Matchett Jas
19 Morgan Rt. stevedore
21 Welsh Jas. seaman
23 Kilpatrick Saml. labourer
25 Anglesey Wltr
27 Ashton Oliver timber labourer
29 Gore Thos. labourer
31 Hindley Mrs. Florence
33 Newton Wm. Jas
35 Cooper Mrs. Margt
37 Lewis Jn. Chas. seaman
39 Williams Rt
41 Whelan Wm
43 Harrison Albt

Rainford av

RIGHT SIDE.
Abbott drive

2 Tomlinson Christphr. labourer
4 Lawson Ernest
6 McClelland Jn. Jas. labourer

the same time as the Beatles where he struck up a friendship with them, and in particular John Lennon. His elder brother Ron acted as a roadie driving the band to the various venues. Back in Liverpool he eventually changed his backing group and linked up with the Manchester based band the Dakotas. He then inserted the letter J into his stage name, at John Lennon's suggestion who felt that it made the name more suitable for a pop singer. As Billy J Kramer and the Dakotas he enjoyed huge success under the management of Brian Epstein and they recorded several songs written by Lennon and McCartney. Epstein had paid Billy's previous manager Ted Knibbs £25 to secure his contract.

Their first hit single 'Do You Want To Know A Secret' reached number two in 1963 in the UK charts and two number one hits followed shortly afterwards. They also enjoyed success in the USA. To his eternal regret, Billy had the opportunity to record 'Yesterday' but turned it down telling Paul McCartney that he preferred a rock'n'roll song. In 1964 the mayor of Bootle held a reception for him at Bootle Town Hall in St John's Road, although he let it be known that Billy's was not the sort of music that he appreciated! In 1965 Billy had a minor scare when he had his tonsils removed at Park House Clinic, Park Road,Crosby but fortunately his voice was not affected. He went solo in January 1967. Now living in the U.S.A, Billy is still in huge demand on both sides of the Atlantic. As well as performing in his own right he is a regular guest at various Beatles conventions when he recounts his memories of his friendship with the Fab Four. A recovering alcoholic he acts as a counsellor to those with drink problems. He speaks to his family in Liverpool each week on the telephone always anxious hear of what is going on in his home town.

Billy J Kramer before a Cavern gig in the 60's (opposite);
Still enjoying success in the 70's (left).

Anne Josephine Robinson was born on 26 September 1944 and the family home was at 28 St Michael's Road, Blundellsands.

Her father Bernard was a teacher and her mother Anne (nee Wilson) ran a chicken wholesale business from a cellar at 13 Market Street, underneath St John's Market. Anne spent the school holidays helping out in the business at her mother's insistence, which included visiting Stanley Abattoir in Prescot Road, Old Swan where her mother was known as 'The Duchess'.

Later when Anne passed her driving test and had left school she drove a van making deliveries all round the Liverpool and Wirral areas. The family were prosperous and regularly had holidays in Cannes staying at the Carlton Hotel.

Happy days at home were spent at the Blundellsands Lawn Tennis Club in Warren Road. Her mother had sent her to Farnborough Hill Convent College in Hampshire to get rid of her Liverpool accent feeling it would jeopardise her future career.

This was followed by finishing school at the Ambassadrices in Paris. She also attended the Shelagh Elliot Clarke School of Dance and Drama at 63 Rodney Street for speech training.

On leaving school she worked briefly as a shorthand typist before embarking on a career in journalism which included spells at the Liverpool Echo and many of the national newspapers including eight years at The Sunday Times.

In 1967 as a young reporter working for a news agency she scooped the story of Brian Epstein's death from a family friend who was the solicitor acting for the Epstein family which helped to secure her a permanent position with the Daily Mail.

She commenced drinking heavily in the 1970s and is a self-confessed recovering alcoholic.

In the 1980s she moved into radio and TV work presenting programmes such as 'Points of View' and 'Watchdog'.

In recent times she is best known for her domineering manner when presenting the TV quiz show' The Weakest Link'. A similar version of the show was broadcast in the USA.

Anne claims to have inherited her forthright manner from her mother who died in 1986. Anne's wink is, however, her own.

Her second marriage of 27 years to John Penrose ended in divorce in 2007. She has homes in London and Gloucestershire.

Her daughter is a top radio and TV presenter in the states.

And here's to you Ms Robinson: young Anne above
Linkwoman - Host of The Weakest Link (BBC); In the 60s (above);
In her home town in the 60s (opposite top).

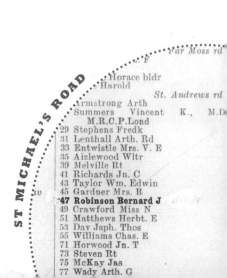

ST MICHAEL'S ROAD

Far Moss rd

Horace bldr
Harold
St. Andrews rd
rmstrong Arth
Summers Vincent K., M.D
M.R.C.P.Lond
29 Stephens Fredk
31 Lenthall Arth. Rd
33 Entwistle Mrs. V. E
35 Aizlewood Wltr
39 Melville Rt
41 Richards Jn. C
43 Taylor Wm. Edwin
45 Gardner Mrs. R
47 Robinson Bernard J
49 Crawford Miss N
51 Matthews Herbt. E
53 Day Jsph. Thos
55 Williams Chas. E
71 Horwood Jn. T
73 Steven Rt
75 McKay Jas
77 Wady Arth. G

ANNE ROBINSON

Anne Robinson, a journalist is now a successful TV star and millionairess. At times a playfully caustic TV presenter, she is famous at home and abroad thanks to her multi award-winning quiz show, The Weakest Link.

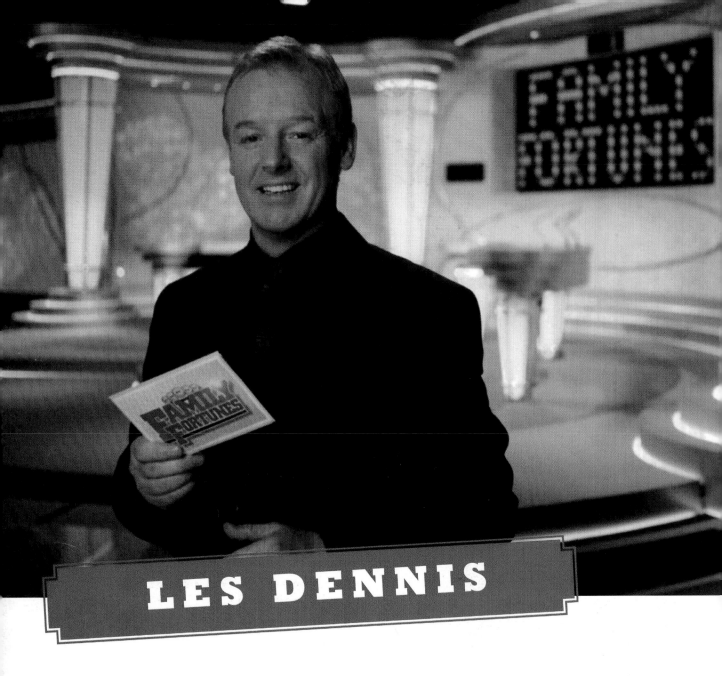

LES DENNIS

Les Dennis comedian, impressionist, actor and ambassador for Liverpool.

Born Leslie Dennis Heseltine on 12 October 1953 the family home was at 83 Chesterton Street, Garston and Les attended Joseph Williams Primary School , Sunnyfield Road, Gateacre and Quarry Bank Grammar School –coincidentally the same primary school as Paul McCartney and the same senior school as John Lennon although both had left by the time Les became a pupil. Leslie though was a contemporary at Quarry Bank of Steve Coppell, the former Tranmere Rovers and Manchester United star and Brian Barwick the former chairman of the Football Association. His father Leslie was a bookmaker and had been on the books of Liverpool Football Club although he did not play for the first team. His mother worked in a local factory. It was his mother who encouraged the young Leslie to pursue a career in show business. Leslie was also a film lover and regularly visited the Odeon Cinema in Allerton Road. He would enter talent competitions whilst on family holidays at Butlins and during his final year at Quarry Bank was appearing at various clubs in Liverpool as a comic. He appeared at the Broadgreen Social Club and the Broadway in Norris Green and later at the Montrose and the Shakespeare. On leaving school Les worked for a short period at Burtons the Tailors and home was now 58 Thornton Road in Childwall and then 'Cromer' in Woolton Hill Road. He came to national attention through TV appearances on ' The Comedians ' and ' New Faces ' and went on to form a successful comedy act with Dustin Gee who died in 1985 whilst appearing in ' Cinderella ' at the Floral Hall in Southport. Les has continued a successful solo career most notably presenting the popular TV quiz show Family Fortunes from 1987- 2002. He also appeared in Brookside and more recently Celebrity Big Brother. He also appears on a regular basis at the Edinburgh Festival.

He has a son Phillip born in 1981 to his first marriage. Les was also married to the actress Amanda Holden for seven years and now lives with his partner Claire Nicholson who is seventeen years his junior.

The couple have a daughter Eleanor Grace who was born in April 2008. In June and July 2008, Les presented four half- hour shows for Granada Television called 'Les Dennis's Liverpool'. Although he left Merseyside in 1987 he often returns home, staying with his sister Marg who lives in Maghull.

One of TV's longest-running hosts of Family Fortunes.
(Above)Sez Les
And on TV in stand-up mode.

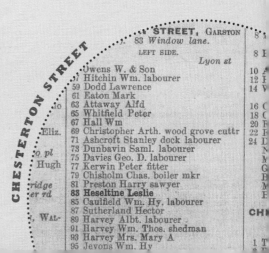

The late great George Melly. Larger than life in colourful clothes and personality to match. Opposite with Jazzkings the Feetwarmers By George we miss people like him.

GEORGE MELLY

George Melly jazz singer, writer, wit, social supremo - and chat show host. He called himself 'Scouse Mouse'.

Born on 17 August 1926 the Melly family has had a long tradition in Liverpool. George's grandfather was linked to the Holts of shipping fame and lived at 90 Chatham Street, Liverpool 7.

His father Tom was a leading businessman whilst his mother, Maud, was involved in amateur dramatic circles.

He grew up with live-in servants and nannies and enjoyed all the trappings of a comfortable middle class home. The family home was at 22 Ivanhoe Road off Lark Lane in Aigburth.

When George was 10 they moved the short distance to 14 Sandringham Drive.

After attending kindergarten in Marmion Road he was sent to a preparatory school in Parkfield Road which he later described as one of the 'unhappiest periods in his life.'

The headmaster Mr W. Twyne was very authoritarian something the young George rebelled against and he was constantly physically disciplined by the headmaster.

Due to his own experiences he was a life-long opponent of corporal punishment in the education system. He completed his education at a public school in Stowe. On leaving school in1944 he served for three

years in the Royal Navy.

He then worked at the London Gallery were he developed his deep love for paintings which remained a passion.

This had begun as a young child in Liverpool with regular visits to the Walker Art Gallery in William Brown Street. Jazz, though, was his first love and he sang with various bands and in 1959 was voted as the ' Melody Maker's ' best male jazz singer. He can also claim to having played at the Cavern Club before the Beatles. George continued to perform for the next five decades and also wrote numerous articles and books including the Flook cartoons in the Daily Mail with Wally Fawkes under the joint name of Trog.

He never forgot his Liverpool roots and returned numerous times including an appearance at a charity concert at the Liverpool Empire in 1984 to show solidarity for the striking miners.

Following a long illness George sadly died on 5 July 2007 but in keeping with the trouper that he was, he continued performing almost to the end of his life.

On Sunday June 10 he appeared at the 100 Club in London at a fund- raising benefit the charity supporting his carers.

SANDRINGHAM DRIVE

wde Thos
Roberts O. W
Dyson Jsph

12 Barwood Hy
12 Isaac Mrs. Edith
12 Smith Eric G
12 Moreton Wm
12 Barlow Edwin A
12 Poland Wm
12 Clay Lloyd
14 Melly Thos

York m

Alexandra dr

SANDRINGHAM ROAD, Old
(13). Lisburn lane.

LEFT SIDE.
3 Snoddon Miss Margt
5 Casey Jas

DEREK NIMMO

Derek Nimmo was a much loved star of stage and screen. The Liverpudlian actor made a great success of playing bumbling clerics such as monks and priests in major TV sitcoms.

Derek was born on 19 September 1930, the only son of Harold and Marjorie. The family home was at 20 Craigmore Road, Mossley Hill.

Derek's father, who died in 1960, worked for the State Assurance Company in Brunswick Street as a clerk. Derek's schooling was spent firstly at Booker Avenue Primary and then at Quarry Bank Grammar the same school as John Lennon, but not at the same time, Derek being ten years his senior.

Because of the war family outings were restricted to Otterspool Promenade and the Cast Iron Shore.

From an early age he displayed an interest in the theatre and visited the Playhouse with his parents whenever he could.

He also ran dances on Saturday nights at St Barnabus Church Hall in Penny Lane.

In the school holidays he went potato picking to earn money to attend speech and drama classes and at the age of sixteen he was offered a part in a London play but his parents refused him permission because they felt he was too young.

Instead he followed in his father's footsteps and secured employment as a clerk with the Road Transport and General Insurance Company in Tower Buildings, 22 Water Street opposite the Liver Building. Around this time he wrote a story ' The Little Apple Tree ' which was published in the Liverpool Echo.

On completing his National Service in 1952, which he had served in Cyprus and Egypt, he joined Goodlass Wall, and Company in Speke selling paint. Shortly afterwards he got his first stage job at the Hippodrome in Bolton and his acting career went from strength to strength resulting in a variety of roles.

He made a cameo appearance in the Beatles film 'A Hard Day's Night' when he played the part of Leslie Jackson a magician with doves.

He is probably best remembered for his portrayal of Brother Dominic in 'Oh Brother' and as the Reverend Mervyn Noote in 'All Gas and Gaiters'.

He was awarded Showbusiness Personality of the Year in 1971.

He had married Patricia Brown on 9 April 1955 at Mossley Hill Parish Church and they had three children Amanda, Timothy and Piers. Derek died of pneumonia in Chelsea and Westminster Hospital on 24 February 1999 following a fall at his London home.

He was 68 years of age. He is buried in the churchyard at Easton Maudit a small rural village in Northamptonshire where he also owned a home.

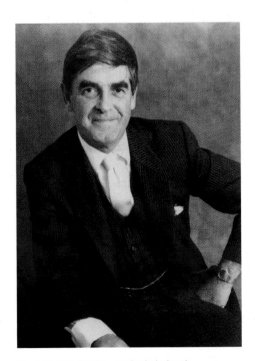

Derek Nimmo Caption - not in clerical garb.
He made his name playing clerical errors.

CRAIGMORE ROAD

th. plumber
rs. Mary B-
rs Leslie Arnold
Couteur K. J
Whiting Fras. Wm. Jsph

RIGHT SIDE.
2 Smith Jn. Elwyn
4 Redhead Herbt. Stephen
6 Higgins Wm. G
8 Fowler Albt. Chas
10 Bos Capt. M. H
12 Lindon Miss Christina
14 Taylor Jn. clerk
16 Smith Chas. Hy. piano tuner
20 Nimmo Hy. clerk

CRAIGS ROAD, OLD SWAN (13).
2 Knoclaid road.

LEFT SIDE.
1 Tharme Jn. Stanley coal mer
3 Fay Wm. cooper
9 Helme Jsph. insur. agt
11 Harrison Jas

DANIEL CRAIG

Daniel Craig's love of theatre began at the Everyman Theatre on Hope Street and it was on one such visit at the age of six he decided that he wanted to become an actor. He is now James Bond.

The sixth actor to play James Bond, Daniel Wroughton Craig was born on 2 March 1968 at 41 Liverpool Road, Chester.

His father Tim was a merchant seaman and later a steel erector. He was also for a while the licensee of the Ring O' Bells Pub near Frodsham.

Daniel's mother Carol was an art teacher with a great interest in the theatre.

She had attended Liverpool Art College and won a place at RADA but did not pursue it. He has one older sister Lea. His parents divorced when he was quite young, his mother eventually remarrying Max Blond and the family moved to Hoylake in 1977, where Daniel lived with his mother and sister and stepfather Max Blond at 9 Valentia Road. His mother had known Max

VALENTIA ROAD

...Nuala C.
...sh, William J.
...ighan, Kezia
...encer, Norah
...Evans, Dorothy M.
...Bird, Phyllis M.
...Sidebottom, Doris
...72 Lewis, Julia M.
...873 Saville, David N.
1874 Saville, Florence R.
1875 Saville, Stephen A.
1876 **Blond, Carol M.**
1877 **Blond, Maxwell**
1878 Roberts, Linda A.
                    GROUND F
1879 Hanlon, Vilma M.   1ST F
1880 Parkinson, Michael J.
1881 Jordan, Anthony D.   T
1882 Jordan, Carolyn E.   T
1883 Jordan, Ian A.   T
1884 Cradduck, Cecilia M.
1885 Cradduck, Donald S.
1886 Boden, Arthur K.
887 Steinmann, Maureen C.
88 Steinmann, Sophie E.

Blond from their Art College days. The family had lived briefly in central Liverpool with Daniel's mother's parents before moving to Hoylake.

His mum would take him with her on her regular visits to the Everyman Theatre in Hope Street and it was on one such visit at the age of six he decided that he wanted to become an actor.

His first school was Frodsham Primary in School Lane, Overton where he regularly appeared in school plays. At the age of nine he transferred to Hoylake Church of England Primary School where he failed the eleven plus and then attended Hilbre High School,Frankby Road, Newton, West Kirby at the same time as Chris Boardman the Olympic cyclist. Whilst at Hilbre Daniel was encouraged to pursue a career in acting by Brenda Davies a teacher at the school. A proficient athlete,and encouraged by his father Tim, Daniel played for Hoylake Rugby Union Club in Melrose Avenue and also Birkenhead Park Colts. From the age of 15 he studied A' Levels at Calday Grange High School in Grammar School Lane, West Kirby but left before taking the examinations.

Andy McCluskey from the band Orchestral Manoeuvres In The Dark also attended Calday.

Daniel left the school two weeks after his sixteenth birthday and shortly after moved to London to study at the National Youth Theatre.

His lifelong acting ambition was soon realised culminating in his portrayal of James Bond in Casino Royale the 21st official Bond film. Divorced he has one daughter,Ella born in 1992 who lives with her mother. Daniel currently lives in London but often refers with fondness to his early Merseyside roots and is a keen supporter of Liverpool Football Club.

Daniel Craig - Merseyside roots - shaken never stirred.

RICKY
TOMLINSON

He started out as a banjo player under the name of, "Hobo Rick'. Stand-up comedy led to acting and he made his name in Brookside- a TV an film career followed.

Ricky was born at Burleigh House, Bispham, Blackpool on 26 September 1939. The second eldest of four boys he was christened Eric but soon everyone would be calling him Rick. His mother Peggy had been evacuated to Blackpool at the outbreak of the Second World War but soon after Rickys birth returned to Liverpool to the family home at 37 Lance Street, close to Liverpool's football ground. Ricky's father Albert was a baker and for 27 years worked nights at Kelly's bakery in nearby Heyworth Street. The young Ricky would spend a lot of time at his grandmothers home in Robsart Street. She was known in the neighbourhood as Fanny Hunter and from all accounts was quite a character. His first school was Heyworth Street Primary and then Breckfield Secondary Modern in Venice Street . Having failed the eleven-plus examination he passed the thirteen plus and enrolled at Walton Technical College on a building trade course. He excelled at plastering and at the age of sixteen started work at Adams Bros, 56 Mason Street, Liverpool 7. In his late teens he began to harbour thoughts of becoming an actor and joined the Bootle Drama Society. He also sang in local pubs and became a proficient banjo player and a stand up comic. He was known as Hobo Rick and wore a huge Stetson hat. In 1962 he left Adams and did freelance plastering work. This was also the year he got married and set up home at 9 Salop Street off Walton Road. Ricky and his wife Marlene then moved to Golborne near Warrington before settling in Wrexham. In 1972 he was sentenced to two years imprisonment for secondary picketing during a national builders strike and was given the Prison number 573143. Ricky and his fellow defendants won a lot of national sympathy for what was perceived as a great injustice but it was 1975 before he was eventually released. He has since of course gone on to achieve national fame in TV shows such as Brookside, Cracker, and Clocking Off but it as Jim Royle the loveable couch potato in the Royle family that he is best known and his comment 'My Arse'! He still lives in Liverpool with his second wife Rita. In 2007 he had a quadruple heart operation at Liverpools Cardithoracic Centre but is now fully recovered and still working hard despite his 70th birthday looming in 2009.

Ricky Tomlisnon (sound as a pound) having a cuppa (opposite). And as Joim Royle in the Royle Family.

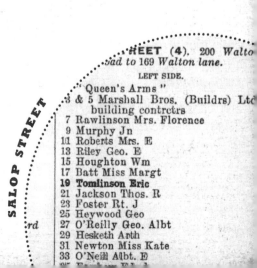

HEET (4). 200 Walto
ad to 169 Walton lane.
LEFT SIDE.
"Queen's Arms "
3 & 5 Marshall Bros. (Buildrs) Ltd
building contrctrs
7 Rawlinson Mrs. Florence
9 Murphy Jn
11 Roberts Mrs. E
13 Riley Geo. E
15 Houghton Wm
17 Batt Miss Margt
19 Tomlinson Eric
21 Jackson Thos. R
23 Foster Rt. J
25 Heywood Geo
27 O'Reilly Geo. Albt
29 Hesketh Arth
31 Newton Miss Kate
33 O'Neill Albt. E

Cilla Black, pop star
turned TV
presenter. Star of
the sixties whom
Brian Epstein
predicted would
be a major TV
celebrity.

CILLA BLACK

Born on 27 May 1943 in Stanley Hospital, she was christened Priscilla Maria Veronica White. She had a younger brother, Alan. The family lived in a flat in Scotland Road which was above George Murray's barbers shop.

Her father worked on the docks and her mother had a stall in St Martins Market.

Cilla as she was always called attended St Anthony's Catholic Junior and Secondary Modern Schools in Newsham Street leaving at the age of fourteen to undertake a typing course at Anfield Commercial College in Belmont Road.

At the age of twenty she was a Dictaphone typist at the BICC Cable Company at 19 Stanley Street which was close to the Cavern Club in Mathew Street which Cilla would visit in her lunch breaks.

In the evenings she acted as a cloakroom attendant at the Cavern and also worked part time at the Zodiac Coffee bar in Duke Street where she met her future husband Bobby Willis.

She would occasionally sing with some of the bands including The Big Three, Kingsize Taylor and The Dominoes and Rory Storm. Her main numbers were 'Fever', 'Always', 'Boys' and 'Summertime'.

Twice Kenny Ball offered her an audition but she got cold feet and turned him down. Various other offers were made to her including a trip to Germany but she refused. It was whilst singing at the Majestic Ballroom in Conway Street, Birkenhead that she was spotted by Brian Epstein who signed her up to his stable of acts.

Brian suggested that she change her surname from White to Black which at first did not go down well with her father.

However, Mr White had years earlier purchased a piano from the Epstein family store in Walton Road, and had been so impressed with the service he had received, that Brian was able to persuade him that it was for the good of his daughter's future career in show business.

A wise decision as Cilla went from strength to strength firstly as a singer with numerous hit records including two number ones, and then as an all round family entertainer with several popular TV shows, Blind Date and Surprise Surprise probably being the most famous.

Bobby and Cilla were married at Marylebone Registery Office on 25 January 1969 with another ceremony taking place at St Mary's Catholic Church in Woolton later on. Bobby sadly passed away on 23 October 1999.

The couple had three sons Robert, Ben and Jack.

Cilla lives in Denham, Surrey in a house that stands in 17 acres of land. After many years absence from the pantomime scene she is due to appear at the Liverpool Empire in December 2008 as part of the Capital of Culture celebrations and a new TV show for Sky TV.

Cilla Black in the 60s (opposite)
Home is where the heart is below on Scottie Road and with Ma.

SCOTLAND ROAD

Kew st
The) Benefit and Thrift
ciety (St. Anthony's branch)
Thos. Casse
iverman Henry wardrobe dealer
Court No. 10
, 372 & 374 "Half Way House" P.H
Mrs. Annie Fitzgerald
Bostock st
376 "Europia (The)" Jn. Duffy
378 Lee Joe laundry
380 **Murray Geo. H. hairdrssr**
382 Ruddock John R. builder
384 & 386 Midland Bank, Ltd. (branch
Dennis Matthew Wilson manage
William Moult st
388 Law Mrs. Frances baker
394 Beardwood Herbt. cycle dlr
Taliesin st
Louis st

BRIAN
EPSTEIN

Brian Epstein, Beatles manager he also successfully looked after Gerry and The Pacemakers, The Four Most and Cilla Black.

The suave Beatles manager was born in a private nursing home at 4 Rodney Street on 19 September 1934.

The building is now administrative offices for the University of Liverpool.

He lived with his parents Harry and Malka, known as Queenie, and younger brother Clive at 157 Queens Drive, Childwall.

Brian spent a lot of his childhood with his grandparents at 27 Anfield Road where he had his own nursery. This is now a guest house which welcomes Beatles fans and visitors to the city from around the world.

A plaque outside serves as the only public recognition of Brian's contribution to the city.

The family business, the first Nems, was founded by his grandfather Isaac and situated at 62-72 Walton Road. Isaac had arrived in Liverpool in 1901 as an immigrant from Lithuania with little money but soon established his own business.

He initially lived at 88 Anfield Road. The shop was demolished in the 1970s and a housing development is now in its place.

Brian started employment there as a window dresser.

He was educated at a variety of schools including Liverpool College.

In the early 1960s he rented a flat at 37 Falkner Street, Liverpool 8 and it was here that John Lennon and Cynthia spent their wedding night. Brian socialised in Liverpool City centre in the fifties and early 60s with his friend and associate Joe Flannery enjoying visits to the Royal Court Theatre.

His favourite watering hole was the Beehive in Paradise Street and he would have his hair cut at Horne Brothers opposite.

The famous NEMS record store which he managed was at 12-14 Whitechapel and was opened in 1957 to compliment the other branch which was based at 50 Great Charlotte Street and where Brian had previously worked.

It was whilst managing the Whitechapel store that he first heard of the Beatles. As well as the Beatles, Brian successfully managed numerous other stars including Gerry and the Pacemakers The Four Most and Cilla Black. Ironically Brian preferred classical music with which his fascination commenced following a visit with his mother to a Liverpool Philharmonic Orchestra concert in 1945.

Brian Epstein was found dead at his London home on 27 August 1967. He was just three weeks short of his 33rd birthday. He is generally recognised as the person responsible for the Beatles remarkable achievements having taken a gamble on them when they were just one of numerous bands in Liverpool.

He is buried in the Jewish Cemetery, Long Lane, Aintree in grave H12, Section A.

The Beatles couldn't have done it without Eppy(opposite) Smiling at success.

QUEENS DRIVE

...tone J. P. & Co. accntnts
...llis Alfd. & Co. insur. brkrs
...ivlin Sol. clothing mfr
  Caplan Mrs. Ettie
89 Caplan Abraham director
191 Dougherty Danl. J
193 Nickson Harry bedstead mfr
195 Rayner Max costumier
197 Epstein Harry house furnisher
199 Dutch David
201 Holden Mrs. Margt. Annie
203 Shaw Wm. Edwin
205 Bell Fredk. Herbt. tea mer
207 Fagin Abraham
209 Crystal Maurice
211 Larrinaga Niceto de Jn
  Dunbabin

LIVERPOOL

This book covers North and South Liverpool as well as Bootle, Huyton and the Wirral.

In my research I have attempted to ascertain which area has produced the most musicians,comics, writers,sports stars.

It is impossible to provide conclusive evidence as each area has had its share of a variety of talents.

However as a general 'rule of thumb'I feel that North Liverpool and Bootle have come up with the greater number of comedians whilst South Liverpool boasts more musicians and writers.

My own theory on my travels is that North Liverpool had the greater number of working men's clubs and dock workers renowned for their humour whilst the South – particularly Liverpool 8 with its cosmopolitan lifestyle and close proximity to the university – is an environment that encourages the more artistic element to blossom.

With the notable exception of Paul O'Grady, the Wirral had produced few comedians but several stars of stage and screen.

Mind you,they say that you have to be a comedian to live there.I should know having resided over the water since 1982.

Only Joking, Wirralonians!

And did you know that for some unknown reason Huyton has created several outstanding writers for tv and screen - must be something in the water.

MERSEYBEAST
A Musical Memoir £8.99

Ian McNabb, is a former leader of Liverpool band Icicle Works and successful solo performer. He is one of Liverpool's finest singer-songwriters as well as being a Mercury Music Prize nominated artist.Ian is the 'Merseybeast' of the title in this, his candid biography, an intimate no-holds-barred guide to the life of a rock and roller – packed with hilarious incidents about Ian's tours, recordings and socialising with the rich and famous. There are many poignant stories, too.It features the highs and lows of this star's roller coaster world packed with photographs from his own archives and enough anecdotes to keep you gripped from his arrival in the music scene to Top of The Pops fame and now as an elder Scouse statesman of rock.The foreword is by BBC's Janice Long.Merseybeast – A Musical Memoir is a 'behind the scenes' pass to McNabb's unique life and it's stamped 'Access all areas.'

MACCA
The Saint and the
Screen Goddess £8.99

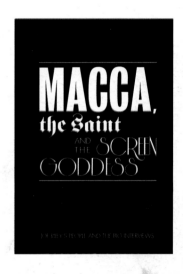

Journalist Joe Riley is one of the Liverpool Echo's longest-serving writers. Joe has interviewed some of the biggest names in the worlds of music – classical and pop – as well as the icons of stage, film and politics.There are revealing chats with icons Paul McCartney and Yoko Ono to his own heroes such as Bob Dylan and Hollywood legend Lauren Bacall.Joe's incisive arts reviews over three decades show what he thought about the first nights of many major productions that went on from Liverpool to the West End and Broadway. But there's also insights into the ordinary yet extraordinary people he has met such as a Merseyside woman who had stigmata.This is the cream of regional journalism from one of the insiders.And TV superstar Jean Boht comes forward with the foreword.Joe says Liverpool is his "news patch' – one of the most vibrant in the UK to work in – if not the world."

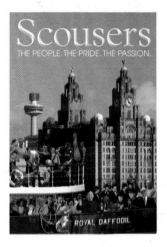

SCOUSERS
£20.00

If there was an encyclopaedia of those people who give 'Scouse' a good name then this hardback book is it.Lavishly illustrated, there are profiles of Scousers – past, present and future.There are glorious photographs from the archives of the Daily Post and Echo and in-depth profiles on Scousers who helped shape the face of the city's architecture, sport, comedy, music and so much more.Scousers is a must for anyone who is proud of the European Capital of culture.This book is not only a celebration of Scouse people but the famous dish and the accent.It redefines the image of this city of amazing contrasts.Scousers is an enjoyable directory of Scousers and Scouse achievement. A 200 page souvenir of a remarkable city.Tom O'Connor and Stan Boardman's passionate forewords welcome you to a magical history story.

THE BEATLES
The Fab Four £3.99

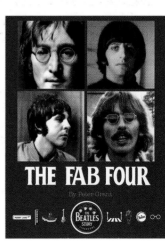

How do you tell the great rock and roll story ever told in 92 pages?Peter Grant, a journalist and a lecturer on The Beatles, has done just that with a publication that is a whistle stop tour through Moptop mania.How did John, Paul, George and Ringo come together to become the most famous quartet on the planet?Tracing their early days in Liverpool to global domination, the book is packed with rare photographs,eye witness accounts and interviews with Paul McCartney and Ringo Starr on special home-comings.The is a celebration of Four likely lads - the Fab Four who shook the world and continue to keep Liverpool firmly on the music map thanks to their global legacy."This is The Beatle story accessible to all ages," said the Daily Post.

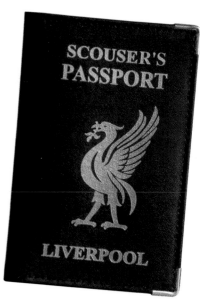